232.5

I Believe in the Resurrection of Jesus

THE VICKRUCK
COLLECTION
OF FINE BOOKS

D1167100

By the same author :

CRUCIAL QUESTIONS ABOUT THE KINGDOM OF GOD

THE BLESSED HOPE

THE NEW TESTAMENT AND CRITICISM

THE PATTERN OF NEW TESTAMENT TRUTH

JESUS AND THE KINGDOM; 2ND REV. ED., THE
    PRESENCE OF THE FUTURE

A THEOLOGY OF THE NEW TESTAMENT

I Believe in the Resurrection of Jesus

by

GEORGE ELDON LADD

WILLIAM B. EERDMANS PUBLISHING COMPANY
Grand Rapids

Copyright © 1975 by George Eldon Ladd. First Printed 1975 for Hodder and Stoughton Limited, London. This American edition by special arrangement with Hodder and Stoughton Ltd.

All Rights Reserved.

Printed in the United States of America.

First printing, July 1975
Second printing, December 1976

Library of Congress Cataloging in Publication Data

Ladd, George Eldon, 1911–
    I believe in the resurrection of Jesus.

    (I believe; no. 2)
    Includes index.
    1. Jesus Christ — Resurrection. 2. Resurrection — Biblical teaching. I. Title.
BT481.L25   232'.5   75-14148
ISBN 0-8028-1611-8

Contents

Editor's Preface

AT THE HEART of Christianity is a cross; and one of the most significant things about it is that it is an empty cross. Christians down the ages have been sure that his shameful death on that gallows was not the last word about Jesus. He rose from the tomb, and triumphed over death.

This was the belief that turned heartbroken followers of a crucified rabbi into the courageous witnesses and martyrs of the early church. This was the one belief that separated the followers of Jesus from the Jews and turned them into the community of the resurrection. You could imprison them, flog them, kill them, but you could not make them deny their conviction that "on the third day he rose again". The resurrection of Jesus Christ from the dead is the cornerstone of Christianity. Every year thousands of enquirers examine the evidence for it and put their faith in Jesus. Every year books come out seeking to discredit it.

It is a matter of the utmost importance. Are we to take seriously Jesus' claims to reveal God? Is there a life beyond the grave? Is forgiveness a beggar's refuge or a genuine possibility? Has history a goal? These are some of the issues which hang on whether or not that crucified rabbi's body still lies rotting in some long forgotten Palestinian grave.

It has recently become fashionable to have one's cake and eat it on this matter of the resurrection. Theologians have been asserting that it does not matter whether Jesus was physically raised from the dead or not: in some sense he still lives. Are they right? Would the early Christians have hailed Jesus as the risen one if they knew perfectly well that he was lying in his grave? How good is the evidence, in any case? These are some of the matters to which Professor Ladd turns his attention in his book. He needs no introduction in scholarly New Testament circles on either side of the Atlantic. Well known as one of the leading New Testament scholars in the U.S.A., he is scarcely less well known in Britain through the publication of his *Jesus and the Kingdon* and *The New Testament and Criticism*. He is singularly well equipped to examine and assess the biblical evidence on this cardinal issue of the Christian faith. He has written a book of striking clarity, and I am confident that it will be widely read both inside and outside scholarly circles.

Michael Green
St. John's College,
Nottingham.

PENTECOST, 1974

CHAPTER I

Introduction

CAN A "MODERN MAN" actually believe in the resurrection of Jesus of Nazareth from the grave? This apparently simple question is one of the most perplexing problems confronting the modern Christian.

Unquestionably the modern man has a different world view in many respects from the first-century Christians. The first century was very familiar with the supernatural and was not troubled by alleged supernatural events. A popular Hellenistic philosopher, contemporary of Jesus, was Apollonius of Tyana, who went about teaching his disciples and performing many alleged miracles. His life was written by one Philostratus. Describing his death, Philostratus writes that Apollonius went into the temple of Dictynna, a Greek goddess. The doors of the temple opened wide to receive him. "And when he had passed within they closed afresh, as if they had been shut, and there was heard a chorus of maidens singing from within the temple, and their song was this, 'Hasten thou from earth, hasten thou to Heaven, hasten.' In other words: 'Do thou go upwards from earth.' "[1] Eusebius tells us that for reasons like these, Apollonius was considered by many to be a divine man.[2]

No modern scholar takes this story seriously; and most think that Apollonius was a charlatan and a quack.[3]

Why should we value any more highly the stories of Jesus' resurrection from the dead than the story of Apollonius' alleged ascension? Is the resurrection of Jesus a historical event? Is it an event in any sense of the word? Or is it merely the expression of early Christian faith in Jesus as a divine man?

To such questions serious scholars have given various answers. Stephen Neill has written, "Christianity is a historical religion in every sense in which this expression can be interpreted."[4] Although Neill is concerned more with the question of the historical Jesus than with the resurrection, since the resurrection, as we shall show, is the most important doctrine of the New Testament, we must assume that Neill means to include the resurrection in this sweeping statement.

My own beloved colleague, Daniel Fuller, has published a book whose central argument is that the resurrection is a real event in the historical past and therefore must be subject to historical verification. The alternative to proof by objective evidences is "a leap into the void".[5] Fuller argues that the historical evidences which prove the resurrection are obvious for all to see. The reason that all men do not see them is the sinful blindness of the human heart. Only the man of faith can see the facts of history. This leads him to say, "History itself is not sufficient to produce faith."[6] Faith can be created only by the grace of God. When one has such faith, "he will be willing to own up to the persuasiveness of the historical evidence."[7] This sounds as though there were two kinds of historical evidences: those which are seen by all men, including unbelievers, and those which can be apprehended only by believers.[8]

A second answer to this problem is supported by scholars who hold that the resurrection was a *real event* in past history but whose nature is such that it transcends history and therefore is not subject to strict verification. One of the most stimulating modern books on the resurrection goes to considerable length to establish "the reality of the resurrection"; but it also says, "The resurrection of Jesus is clearly rooted in history, although it is not in itself a historical fact."[9] "The reality of the resurrection of Jesus lies beyond our earthly categories."[10] It is "a primal miracle beyond the bounds of the immanent world".[11]

A recent British scholar, discussing Paul's witness to Jesus' resurrection in 1 Corinthians 15, writes, "The only part of this statement which can be said to be capable of historical verification is the existence of the belief that the event had actually occurred, and Paul goes on to give a list of people who claimed to have 'seen' Jesus alive after his death, among whom he includes himself. The existence of the belief, therefore, is one of the unshakable things; but the event itself and the statement that it took place on the third day after the death of Jesus cannot be historically verified. If the event called the resurrection of Jesus is to be accepted as one of the things which cannot be shaken, it must be on other grounds than historical verification."[12]

In the same vein, an American scholar writes, "It was not a 'historical', but an eschatological and meta-historical event occurring precisely at the point where history ends, but leaving its mark in history negatively in the empty tomb . . . and positively in the appearances."[13]

What are we to make of such statements? Is it possible for an event to occur in history and yet not be fully historical? Can events take place in the past which are not subject to historical verification? Can such scholars who deny the full historicity of the resurrection be said really to believe in the reality of the resurrection? Are not such statements a thin cloak which really hides unbelief?

Before we deal with such questions, a third answer to the resurrection must be given. Some scholars firmly deny the facticity of the resurrection if it means the restoration of a dead man to life. Probably the bluntest statement of this sort comes from Rudolf Bultmann who affirms flatly, "A historical fact which involves a resurrection from the dead is utterly inconceivable."[14] Whether or not we agree with Bultmann, we should appreciate his unambiguous candour. While denying the past historicity of the resurrection, Bultmann insists that he retains the true *meaning* of the resurrection. "Christ meets us in the preaching as one crucified and risen. He meets us in the word of preaching and nowhere else. The faith of Easter is just this faith in the word of preaching."[15] In a more recent writing, he states the same truth: "According to my interpretation of the kerygma, Jesus has risen in the kerygma."[16]

Perhaps Bultmann's position and that of such scholars as Künneth, Hooke and Fuller will appear to the reader to be the same in that they both deny the "historicity" of the resurrection. This, however, is not the case. Künneth, Hooke and Fuller recognise the resurrection as an *event* which happened *in* past history but whose nature is such that it is not subject to control by the ordinary means of historical verification. To illustrate: Hooke notes the differences between Jesus in the flesh and the resurrected Jesus. "He does not return to the ordinary life and daily companionship with his disciples, but appears and disappears in a way which does not conform to the mode of normal earthly existence in time and space."[17] Again, he says, "We are confronted by an event whose nature, like that of the Incarnation of the Word, places it beyond and outside the world where natural causes operate."[18] The resurrection is an event "whose character places it beyond the world where what we call natural causes operate".[19] Hooke fully recognises the eventfulness — the facticity of the resurrection; but its nature is such that it cannot be explained by the ordinary historical laws of cause and effect. Every "historical" event must have a "historical" cause. The resurrection of Jesus was an act of God, unmediated by any other historical event. Furthermore, as we shall see, Jesus' resurrection was not a return to physical earthly life; *it was the emergence within history of the life of the world to come.* What can a historian as historian say about the world to come? This is a dimension that belongs to faith. This is why Hooke insists that "as Christians, we accept his resurrection, not on the ground of historical evidence, but on the ground of faith".[20] We will deal with this problem later.

It is the thesis of this book that there must be interaction between historical evidences and faith. Faith is not a blind leap in the dark without any historical evidences. Neither will historical evidences *demand* faith, for the man of unbelief will always come up with different historical explanations. However, faith is supported and reinforced by historical evidences.

Why, then, should Bultmann flatly deny the facticity of the resurrection as an event in past history?[21]

The answer to this is suggested by Willi Marxsen who introduces a short essay on the resurrection by noting that the modern scholar's view of history is controlled by principles which came out of the Enlightenment. "We must now simply acknowledge that the scientific study of history, too, has its own methodology."[22] This "scientific methodology" is one which *a priori* excludes the possibility of divine acts in history. It has laid down in advance the limits of historical study. It assumes that history is a closed continuum, that all historical events must have historical causes. It assumes an unbroken chain of cause and effects in the flow of history. The Enlightenment assumed that human reason and observation were the measures of all historical reality. Thus the "scientific" method excludes the possibility of the supernatural before it has studied the evidence. It is based on a philosophical presupposition about the nature of historical reality.

This utterly anti-miraculous, naturalistic approach to the biblical history is supposed to be more "scientific" and "objective" than a method that recognises the reality of the supernatural. However, the exact opposite may be true. A truly scientific method is the inductive method which accepts as a working hypothesis the *best explanation for the known facts*. There are certain known "historical" facts which we will shortly discuss: the death and burial of Jesus; the discouragement and disillusionment of the disciples; their sudden transformation to be witnesses to Jesus' resurrection; the empty tomb; the rise of the Christian church; and the conversion of Saul. The "historical method" must come up with a satisfying, convincing "historical" explanation for this set of facts. It is our contention that no such historical explanation has yet been produced, and that the best hypothesis to account for the known "facts", indeed, the only adequate hypothesis, is that God raised Jesus from the dead in bodily form. However, the so-called "scientific" method excludes the possibility of this hypothesis at the very outset. Far from being open-minded and "objective", it is closed-minded to one of the most viable explanations. If there is a living God who is the Lord of history, who has chosen to act in historical events as the Bible witnesses, the "scientific method" has no way of recognising that fact. On the contrary, the very presuppositions of the scientific method makes it blind to one very live option. In other words, the scepticism of such scholars as Bultmann and Marxsen is not due to problems which arise as a result of an inductive study of the texts; it is due rather to the presupposition that a literal bodily resurrection to which our Gospels witness is excluded. The man of faith is therefore more open-minded than the so-called scientific historian.

In this book we propose to use the inductive historical method of study rather than the "scientific" historical-critical method.

We must first appreciate the importance of the doctrine of resurrection.[23] We must make clear the problem of faith and history that so much colours the contemporary discussion. Then our primary task is to try to *explain the rise of the resurrection faith*. We must thoroughly canvass the Old Testament, contemporary Judaism, as well as the New Testament to see if there are to be found ideas which can account for the rise of the resurrection faith. We must carefully analyse the witness of the New Testament to define as clearly as possible the nature of the resurrection. We must also survey modern "historical" explanations for the rise of the resurrection faith. Finally, we must evaluate the importance of the resurrection fact for the totality of the biblical revelation.

NOTES

1. See Philostratus, *The Life of Apollonius of Tyana* (Loeb Classical Library. New York: Macmillan, 1912), II, 401.
2. *Ibid.*, II, 507.
3. See *Smith's Smaller Classical Dictionary* (New York: Dutton, 1940), p. 57.
4. Stephen Neill, *The Interpretation of the New Testament 1861–1961* (London: Oxford, 1964), p. 342.
5. Daniel P. Fuller, *Easter Faith and History* (Grand Rapids: Eerdmans, 1965), p. 256.
6. *Ibid.*, p. 237.
7. *Loc. cit.*
8. Fuller would deny that there are two kinds of history. He would insist there is only one kind of history, but the unbelieving mind cannot really see what is *there*.
9. Walter Künneth, *The Theology of the Resurrection* (London: S.C.M., 1965), p. 60.
10. *Ibid.*, p. 78.
11. *Ibid.*, p. 80.
12. S. H. Hooke, *The Resurrection of Christ* (London: Darton, Longman and Todd, 1967), p. 107.
13. Reginald H. Fuller, *The Formation of the Resurrection Narratives* (New York: Macmillan, 1971), p. 48.
14. Rudolf Bultmann, *Kerygma and Myth* (London: S.P.C.K., 1953), I, 39.
15. *Ibid.*, p. 41.
16. See Carl E. Braaten and Roy A. Harrisville, *The Historical Jesus and the Kerygmatic Christ* (New York: Abingdon, 1964), p. 42.
17. S. H. Hooke, *op. cit.*, p. 111.
18. *Ibid.*, p. 112.
19. *Ibid.*, p. 113.

20. *Ibid.*, p. 110.
21. Bultmann would say that the resurrection is an *event* in past history. Jesus rose in the kerygma—the preaching of the living Christ in the apostolic church. The resurrection continues to be an event as the hearer is confronted by the proclaimed word of the resurrected Saviour. The only "historical" event connected with past history is the rise of the faith in the risen Lord. (*Op. cit.*, p. 42.)
22. See *The Significance of the Message of the Resurrection for Faith in Jesus Christ* (London: S.C.M., 1968), p. 17.
23. We call it a doctrine rather than a historical fact for reasons which will emerge later.

CHAPTER 2

Faith and History

THE VERY TITLE of this book suggests a host of questions which are vigorously debated in contemporary theology. Is the resurrection of Jesus a postulate of faith or a historical fact? This is a question one cannot dismiss lightly. An uncritical view accepts everything the Bible relates as simple forthright history. However, a moment's reflection shows that there is a valid and necessary distinction between faith and history. Faith has to do with the invisible world of God; history has to do with the empirical world of men and things. God is not a historical character. The Christian *believes* in the God revealed in the Bible, and he *believes* that he talks to God in prayer and that God speaks to him through his Word and his Spirit. But he has never seen God with his eyes as he has seen other people; he has never felt God's hand as he feels the handshake of his friend; he never hears the voice of God with his physical ears as he hears the voice of his neighbour. "No one has ever seen God" (Jn. 1:18).

As a matter of fact, the Bible nowhere tries to *prove* the existence of God. God's existence is everywhere assumed. "Now faith is the assurance of things hoped for, *the conviction of things not seen*" (Heb. 11:1). "For whoever would draw near to God must believe that he exists and that he rewards those who seek him" (Heb. 11:6).

The realm of God is the object of faith, not sight (2 Cor. 5:1). It is not subject to scientific demonstration nor historical investigation. The scientist as scientist can make no objective statements about God, based on his scientific research. He can philosophise or speculate about first causes and the like, or he can speak out of Christian faith, but he cannot as a scientist say anything positively or negatively about God and the world of God. As a historian, he can speak of men's belief in God, but he cannot speak of God himself, for God stands above all nature and history. To be sure, Paul does say that reason demands faith in the existence of God because of the orderliness of nature (Rom. 1: 19-20), but this is still in the nature of faith, not of scientific demonstration.

However, precisely at this point, the Bible presents us with a problem. The central theme of the entire Bible is that God has acted in historical events. The Bible says that God called Abram out of Haran to Canaan (Gen. 12:1). The historian may be able to say that Abram did indeed go from Haran to Canaan, and that Abram *thought* it was God who had called him to do so; but how can the historian establish that it was God who led Abram to make this migration?

The Bible says that God delivered Israel from bondage in Egypt by the hand of Moses. This was no ordinary event in history like the events which befell the other nations. It was not an achievement of the Israelites. It was not attributed to the genius and skilful leadership of Moses. It was an act of God. "You have seen what I did to the Egyptians, and how I bore you on eagles' wings" (Exod. 19:4).

This deliverance was not merely an act of God; it was an act through which God made himself known and through which Israel was to know and serve God. "I am the Lord, and I will bring you out from under the burdens of the Egyptians, and I will deliver you from their bondage; and *you shall know that I am the Lord your God*" (Exod. 6:6-7).

The historian can establish that the Israelites did indeed escape from Egypt and travel to Canaan under the leadership of Moses, even though the date of that event is still a subject of historical debate; but how can the historian prove that it was God who led them in this deliverance? The traditional orthodox answer might point to the miracles wrought by Moses, but the historian is always able to point to analogous events which are accompanied by legendary accretions, and thus explain away the alleged supernatural.

The same problem inheres in the life and death of Jesus.

According to our Gospels, Jesus was the Son of God incarnate (Mk. 1:1; Jn. 1:14). The Gospels relate that he performed mighty works which testified to the nature of his person. But these works were subject to different interpretations. Jesus' opponents admitted that he possessed supernatural power, but they said it was demonic power (Mt. 12:24). His friends— probably his own family—admitted that he did marvellous deeds, but they thought he was out of his mind (Mk. 3:21). Jesus was the Son of God only to those who responded to him in faith. Today, the historian can read the Gospels and make judgments about what men thought about Jesus and even what Jesus thought about himself; but how can the historian, as a historian, say that Jesus was the Son of God? He might conclude that Jesus *thought* he was the Son of God; but this might mean no more than that Jesus had a "messiah complex" and was deluded.

As to the death of Jesus, the historian stands on firm soil. "Crucified under Pontius Pilate"—here is historical bedrock. Few competent scholars of any theological persuasion today question that fact.

But this is only half of the story. "Christ died"—that is solid history. But Christ died "for our sins" (1 Cor. 15:3). Is that history? Certainly, if it is true, it happened *in history*. But is not the atonement, although it happened in history, an event which can be perceived alone by faith?

To illustrate: Paul says, "God shows his love for us in that while we were yet sinners Christ died *for us*" (Rom. 5:8). This is the one sure evidence of God's love: not God's general providence, not the events of my own life, but one event in history: the death of Christ *for sinners*. But when Jesus died, who saw the love of God in his death? He had been betrayed and forsaken by his disciples. His mother and a few women, together with "the disciple whom Jesus loved" (Jn. 19:26) stood by watching him die. Near the cross, the soldiers gambled. One thief cursed God and man. The other thief prayed as he died. But *who of those* around the cross watching Jesus die was suddenly overtaken with a great sense of God's love? Who was caused to throw himself on the ground with a cry of joy: "I never knew how much God loved me?" No one. The atonement was veiled from the eyes of men. The crucifixion, to all outward appearances—i.e. historically—was a bloody, revolting, cruel tragedy. Here was a good man who became the pawn of power politics, who got caught between the millstones of the church and state—the Sanhedrin and the Roman Prefect—and was deliberately sent by Pilate to an innocent death. Historically, the death of Jesus is sheer tragedy.

But unseen by the eyes of men, he was dying for the sins of the world. Atonement was being accomplished. God in love was giving up his Son (Jn. 3:16). However, this was not evident. It was not known at the time. It was only later understood and accepted as such—as the divinely-provided atonement for human sins. Jesus died: this is solid history. Jesus died *for our sins*: this is the meaning, the interpretation of the historical event which can be seen only by the eyes of faith. In this sense, the atonement is not strictly speaking a historical event. It is the *meaning* of a historical event. It is an act of God, where God acted in history, in the Jesus of history, to redeem the world.

It should be clear from this discussion that the statement that such an event as the atonement is not "historical" does not in any way prejudice the case against its facticity—its having-happenedness—its objectivity. "Objectivity" can mean two different things. It can mean "open to public gaze" and thus be synonymous with "historicity" in the strict sense of the word. It can also mean that it is not merely subjective, in my mind. It really happened "out there". We use objectivity in the second way. The atonement was an objective event which happened at a definite time and in a definite place. But its nature as an act of God was such that it was not open to the public gaze. Although an event in history, it was a transaction between God and Jesus. This is why it had to be interpreted by inspired words to be understood for what it was. The atonement is one of the high points where the world of God intersects the world of man in such a way that "spiritual" events affect the destiny of the whole human race.

This is what may be called the fundamental presupposition of the entire Bible: that there are two worlds—the visible and the invisible—the world of man and the world of God—the natural and the supernatural. However, God is not so transcendent, so "wholly other", that he is aloof from history. God has chosen in one strand of history to effect a redemptive revelation of himself. Sometimes he works in and through ordinary historical events in such a way that his action is altogether hidden from the gaze of men. The atonement is an illustration of this. At other times his actions involve some deviation from the normal course of things. The miracles of Jesus are an illustration of this. The Gospels unanimously witness to the mighty works of Jesus: demon exorcisms, healing miracles, nature miracles, even on two occasions the raising of the dead. No kind of apologetics can *prove* the facticity of such miracles, any more than it can *prove* the virgin birth of Jesus. One believes them or does not believe them largely depending on his view of God and of the relationship of God to history. The Bible everywhere presupposes that God is able to act in history both mediately — in an unseen way, and immediately — in ways which can be seen. However, even the supernatural events need *interpretation* by inspired words to be understood for what they are — the acts of God. Even these acts are open to diverse interpretations, as we have seen in the case of Jesus' own person.

What shall we say about the resurrection of Jesus? Was it a historical event, open to public gaze and historical confirmation? Was it an event like the atonement, hidden from human eyes, understood only by inspired words of interpretation?

That equally evangelical scholars can differ in their interpretation of the relationship of the resurrection to history is illustrated by two essays in the volume *Jesus of Nazareth: Saviour and Lord*.[1] Merrill Tenney, writing on "The Historicity of the Resurrection", argues from the principle of historical cause and effect. "The existence of the church demands a historical cause for its origin."[2] At the same time, he says that "the resurrection entails a transformation of the present body that will fit it for a more glorious existence . . . The resurrection belongs to a world of dimensions different from ours, although it did occur within the bounds of time and space."[3] But what does the historian know about a world of different dimensions from ours? What does he know or what can he say *as a historian* about the world of God or the world to come? We shall deal with the question of cause and effect later. Certainly a historical event needs a cause *adequate* to explain it. In fact, this is the thesis of this book. But must the cause be strictly speaking *historical* in the sense that it is an event open to public view and examination? Cannot God be the cause of events in history? But more of this later.

Clark Pinnock takes a somewhat different tack in his essay "On the Third Day". Discussing the historicity of the resurrection, he appeals to faith. "Faith in the risen Lord arises out of the work of the Spirit in the mind of a man considering the claims of the gospel. The Spirit acts upon evidence to accredit the message. The evidence consists chiefly, as historical evidence does, of the personal testimony of those close to the event."[4] But is *faith* necessary to establish historical facts? Why is the work of the Spirit necessary to convince the mind of an observer or scholar as to the facticity of an alleged event? Pinnock goes on to speak of the resurrection as a miracle. "If at the outset a person excludes the miraculous as a possibility, no amount of persuasion would be sufficient to necessitate belief."[5] Well said. But this is precisely the issue at stake. A miracle is an event *in history* which has *no historical cause*. It is an act of God, not of man. Disbelief in the miracles of Jesus goes hand in hand with disbelief in his deity.

When we pursue further the question of the resurrection and history, the first thing to be noted is that nobody saw Jesus rise from the dead. Mark (16: 14), Luke (24: 2) and John (20: 2) merely report that the women found the stone rolled away from the tomb but found the tomb empty. Matthew (28: 2) reports that there was an earthquake, for an angel of the Lord came down and rolled back the stone. None of our Gospels say, or even hint, that the stone was rolled back to let Jesus out. He was gone when the stone was removed. The stone was rolled back to show that the tomb was empty, that Jesus was not there. Exactly when Jesus rose from the dead we cannot say. How then can Jesus' resurrection in any sense be called a historical event, when there were no witnesses? We do indeed have witnesses to appearances of the risen Lord, and we have witnesses to the empty tomb. We have to agree with Marxsen[6] that the resurrection is an inference drawn from the appearances of Jesus. However, we cannot agree with Marxsen that the resurrection was an inference derived from the personal faith of Peter and the other disciples,[7] or that the resurrection merely revitalised the same faith the disciples had

in Jesus during his ministry.[8] The disciples were not believing.
They had lost hope. Something had to happen to create their
faith. It was not faith which created the experience of the
appearances, but the appearances which created belief in the
resurrection.

Furthermore, our Gospels clearly are not eyewitness
accounts. None of the authors of the Gospels claims to have
seen the resurrected Jesus. Mark was perhaps written around
A.D. 60, a full generation after the events of Jesus' life, and the
other two Gospels at least a decade later. During the inter-
vening generation, the Gospel material was preserved in oral
form.[9] The stories about Jesus were preserved in the church
and handed down from mouth to mouth. Some form critics
maintain that the Gospel tradition was radically transformed
by the faith of the community. In other words, we have no
primary sources for the rise of the resurrection faith. We have
only secondary sources which are a generation removed from
the events they relate. Are they trustworthy? Can I establish
reliable historical events from such records?

If there were no witnesses to the resurrection, if our Gospels
do not purport to give us an eyewitness account of the
resurrection, we are faced with the question, Is the resurrection
a *necessary* inference? Is there not some other historical explanation for the belief in Jesus' resurrection?

At this point we must discuss the nature of the historical
method. What is history? How are historical events established?

A simple uncritical answer would be that "history" is what
has happened. However, such a simplistic view is impossible.
I have no idea of what happened in the past except as it has
been recorded in one way or another. History, then, is the
study of historical records, documents, and the like. However,
such documents and records are not entirely trustworthy.
They reflect legend, exaggeration, and the obvious generous
use of imagination. For instance, the church father Epiphanius
of the fourth century A.D. tells a fantastic story of the translation
of the Hebrew Old Testament into Greek. He tells of how
seventy-two Jewish scribes were shut up in pairs in thirty-six
cells, and each book of the Old Testament given to each pair
in turn to be translated. Thus each book was translated thirty-
six times. When these translations were compared, they were

found to agree exactly. No discrepancies were found to exist between the thirty-six different renditions. This is a highly imaginative story which historically is utterly incredible, especially when it is compared with the very confused character of the extant Greek Old Testament. Ancient records must be studied *critically*. We are driven to the conclusion that *history is the modern historian's effort to reconstruct the past by the critical use of ancient records and documents.*

At this point, it is important to note that the so-called "historical-critical method", especially as it is understood in Germany, is not an open-minded inductive study of the evidence. Rather, ancient literature is studied and past events reconstructed with certain rigid presuppositions of what could or could not have happened. This is done, however, in the name of scientific objectivity. One of America's outstanding New Testament scholars wrote, "Is it not axiomatic that, aside from the assumption that there is order in the universe, critical historical research can brook no theoretical presuppositions? . . . Modern science and philosophy have no place for miracles and special providences. History is the result of the complex interaction of natural and social forces and the actions and reactions of men. There are neither demons nor angels. God acts only through men."[10] While such a statement disclaims any theoretical presuppositions, as a matter of fact, it affirms one basic presupposition: that miracles cannot occur. This positivistic or naturalistic view of history is not an element of Christian tradition but is a product of the rationalism of the Enlightenment. It results from trying to treat history as though it were a natural science. It is to be noted that this historiography is not a product of Christian faith nor of inductive study of the Bible, but of secular reasoning. However, this approach has dominated the methodology of more than a century of New Testament research. It is clearly defined by Rudolf Bultmann, one of the greatest minds of our generation: "The historical method includes the presuppositions that history is a unity in the sense of a closed continuum of effects in which individual events are connected by the succession of cause and effect . . ." We must "understand the whole historical process as a closed unity. This closedness means that the continuum of historical happenings cannot be rent by the interference of supernatural powers and that therefore there is no 'miracle' in this sense of the word. Such a miracle would be an event whose cause did not lie within history."[11] Just so! It is self-evident that this presupposition excludes the Bible's view of God in his relationship to history. Bultmann would cordially agree. He views the Bible's world-view as "mythology" which would involve a *sacrificium intellectus* — a sacrifice of the intellect, and is impossible for the modern man. He is famous for his programme of "demythologisation" which tries to find an existential truth in the biblical myths. This is what leads Bultmann to say that "a historical fact which involves a resurrection from the dead is utterly inconceivable."[12] "If the event of Easter Day is in any sense a historical event additional to the event of the cross, it is nothing else than the rise of faith in the risen Lord . . . All that historical criticism can establish is the fact that the first disciples came to believe in the resurrection."[13] However, as a historian, Bultmann has to account for the rise of the resurrection faith. The disciples *believed* they had seen Jesus alive after his death. They *believed* in the bodily resurrection of Jesus. Here we are on bedrock. It is impossible to question the facticity of the disciples' belief in Jesus' resurrection. What is the *historical* cause of this faith? What historical event caused them to believe that Jesus had risen from the dead?

Here, Bultmann seems to founder. In the essay first quoted, Bultmann offers the explanation, "The historian can perhaps to some extent account for that faith from the personal intimacy which the disciples had enjoyed with Jesus during his earthly life, and so reduce the resurrection appearances to a series of subjective visions."[14] However, it appears that Bultmann is less than satisfied with this explanation, for Thielicke quotes him in another context as taking the position that these visions were not purely subjective, but had an objective basis. The visions are in a real sense objective encounters. What they saw was not imaginary. Their faith was "directed towards an object; though an object which is not purely external to him, but which operates as a reality within him."[15] However, in a later work, Bultmann says that how the Easter faith arose in the disciples has been obscured in the tradition by legend, "and is not of basic importance".[16] Here is an amazing statement. How can it be irrelevant to discover the event that gave rise to one of the most influential movements in Western Civilization? Can Bultmann's agnosticism be due to the fact that the resurrection is precisely this—a miracle—and that there is no natural cause? If the biblical record is true, *there can be no purely historical explanation for the rise of the resurrection faith.* It is due to an act of God which happened *in history* but did not happen in terms of historical causality.

Nevertheless, this naturalistic interpretation of history which excludes *a priori* the possibility of resurrection continues to be widely employed. Thus a brilliant American scholar writes that the possibility of miracles must be excluded from positivistic historiography not because of certain dogmatic presuppositions but because of the demands of the historical method itself.[17] Marxsen admits that the resurrection is a miracle, but he says it is impossible to recognise the miraculous character of an event belonging to the past: "I can at most guess that it was a miracle—but *only* if I am acquainted with the corresponding miracle today."[18] "The miracle is the birth of faith."[19] But are we to limit the freedom of God? Must God always act in the same way? Granted that it is hard to believe in such a miracle as a bodily resurrection *in the light of modern scientific knowledge.* But is God limited to our present experience? The biblical witness is conscious that not only in Jesus' resurrection but also in his entire mission, God has acted in a unique way. What he did in Jesus he did "once and for all" (Heb. 7:27). It should be obvious that to any man who adopts the presuppositions of the historical-critical historiography, the New Testament witness to the resurrection of Jesus is impossible. No amount of evidence can persuade a mind that is closed.

We have thus far discussed two different concepts of history: history as those events open to universal examination; and history as a closed nexus of historical causes and effects. The difference between these two should be obvious; and it is important. For the former, the resurrection can be a real objective event in history even if its nature is such that it cannot strictly speaking be called "historical" because by its very nature it transcends the historical. For the latter, it is a contradiction in terms to speak of an event in history which is not at the same time caused by some antecedent historical event. From this perspective, literal resurrection is impossible.

Miracles do not happen. The only certain historical fact is the rise of the resurrection faith.

If there are events in history whose nature transcends the historical dimension, how can their facticity be established? What kind of historiography can be used? Can faith establish the facticity of past historical events?

Alan Richardson, in his excellent book, *History Sacred and Profane*,[20] has a more inductive method for doing history, particularly with reference to the resurrection of Jesus. "Two conditions would have to be fulfilled before the judgment could be reached that the traces of the past point towards the resurrection of Christ as the most coherent explanation of the evidence. First, there would have to be credible attestation on the part of witnesses to happenings which could not be more rationally accounted for by some alternative hypothesis; and, secondly, the event attested would have to accord with the historian's own deepest understanding and experience of life."[21] By this second condition, Richardson means to say, "he will have to know in his own life something of that self-transcendence which enables men in every age to relive the historic reality of the original Christian community to which the New Testament bears witness. This is what in Christian terminology is called 'faith' . . . Christian theology has never suggested that the 'fact' of Christ's resurrection could be known apart from faith."[22]

In this position, there is an interacting of two factors: historical evidences and faith. By historical criticism, I study the admitted historical facts. How are they to be explained? What could have given rise to the resurrection faith? How do we account for the stories of the empty tomb? Are they credible? Possibly there are promises in the Old Testament which led Jesus' disciples after his death to believe, contrary to the fact, that Jesus was risen from the dead. Possibly there are expectations in contemporary Jewish thought which the disciples shared about the death and resurrection of the Messiah (whom the disciples believed Jesus to be) which will account for their faith. Possibly two thousand years of study and investigation have come up with some adequate explanations for the rise of the resurrection faith. As a historian, I must take all of these possibilities into consideration. But as a *Christian* historian who has met the risen Christ in my inner religious experience, I am open to the possibility that God actually raised Jesus from the dead. I must consider all the possibilities, evaluate all the possible hypotheses, and then choose the explanation which makes the best sense. The present author has to admit that if the historian as such can come up with an adequate *historical*, i.e. natural, explanation for the rise of the resurrection faith, his confidence in the integrity of the New Testament witness to the resurrection would be deeply undermined, if not completely shattered. Thielicke calls this method that of "anti-criticism". It is not possible for historical criticism to *prove* the resurrection. It is the task of anti-criticism to establish that there are no known historical facts which contradict the Easter faith.[23] In other words, the *hypothesis* that Jesus actually rose from the dead is the best hypothesis to account for the known historical facts. How can I accept such a hypothesis? Because, as Richardson says, it agrees with my deepest experience of reality — my experience with the living Christ.

In applying this method, there is an interaction between "historical" evidences and faith. To be sure, the last word belongs to faith. But such faith is not a leap in the dark. It is reinforced by critical study. We may here recall the word of Pinnock: "Faith in the risen Lord arises out of the work of the Spirit in the mind of a man considering the claims of the gospel. The Spirit acts upon the evidence to accredit the message. This evidence consists chiefly, as historical evidence does, of the personal testimony of those close to the event. If at the outset a person excludes the miraculous as a possibility, no amount of persuasion would be sufficient to necessitate belief. The problem, then, concerns not the adequacy of the evidence, but the openness of the man to admit the fact."[24]

It is not the purpose of this book therefore by historical reasoning to prove the resurrection. It is our purpose to establish the thesis that the bodily resurrection of Christ is the only adequate explanation to account for the resurrection faith and the admitted "historical" facts. Thus we hope to show that, for one who believes in the God who has revealed himself in Christ, the resurrection is entirely rational and utterly consistent with the evidences.

NOTES

1. Ed. by C. F. H. Henry (Grand Rapids: Eerdmans, 1966).
2. *Ibid.*, p. 138.
3. *Ibid.*, p. 143.
4. *Ibid.*, p. 153.
5. *Loc. cit.*
6. Willi Marxsen in *The Significance of the Message of the Resurrection for Faith in Jesus Christ* (London: S.C.M., 1968), pp. 15–50.
7. Willi Marxsen, *The Resurrection of Jesus of Nazareth* (Philadelphia: Fortress, 1970), p. 138.
8. *Ibid.*, p. 125.
9. See G. E. Ladd, *The New Testament and Criticism* (Grand Rapids and London: Eerdmans and Hodder and Stoughton, 1967), chap. VI.
10. C. C. McCown, "The Current Plight of Biblical Scholarship," *Journal of Biblical Literature*, 75: (1956) 17f.
11. Rudolf Bultmann, *Existence and Faith*, ed. by Schubert M. Ogden (New York: Meridian Books, 1960), pp. 291–2.
12. Rudolf Bultmann, *Kerygma and Myth*, ed. by H. W. Bartsch (London: S.P.C.K., 1953), p. 39.
13. *Ibid.*, p. 42.
14. *Loc. cit.*
15. As quoted by Helmut Thielicke in *op. cit.*, p. 152.
16. Rudolf Bultmann, *Theology of the New Testament* (New York: Scribners Sons, 1951), I, p. 45.
17. James M. Robinson, *Kerygma und historicher Jesus* (Zürich: Zwingli, 1960), p. 14n.
18. Willi Marxsen, *op. cit.*, p. 113.
19. *Ibid.*, p. 128.
20. London: S.C.M., 1964.
21. *Ibid.*, p. 195.
22. *Ibid.*, p. 206.
23. Helmut Thielicke in Leonhard Goppelt, *et al.*, *The Easter Message Today* (London and New York: Thomas Wilson, 1964), p. 83.
24. Clark H. Pinnock, *Jesus of Nazareth: Saviour and Lord*, p. 153.

CHAPTER 3

The Centrality of the Resurrection

A RECENT SCHOLAR writing on the resurrection says, "To a greater extent than it is anything else, Christianity — at least the Christianity of the New Testament — is a religion of resurrection."[1] Before we engage in a study of the evidences for the resurrection of Jesus and the nature of that event, we should be aware of how much is at stake in the study.

In the first place, it is clear that the four Gospels were written from the perspective of Jesus' resurrection. The Evangelists were confident that Jesus was conscious that his mission would lead him to his death, but that beyond death would be resurrection. We are not now concerned with the question of the authenticity of these words — whether Jesus said them or not. We are only concerned with their existence and the belief of the early church. At the least, they represent early Christian faith. They reflect the fact not only that the early church believed that Jesus had risen from the dead; they believed that Jesus himself believed he would rise from the dead.

The Gospels represent Jesus as being conscious early in his career that an untimely death awaited him. In a passage placed early in Mark, the people came to Jesus with a question, "Why do John's disciples and the disciples of the Pharisees fast but your disciples do not fast?" This is followed by both Matthew and Luke. It is clear from this question that not all of John's disciples had left him to become disciples of Jesus but had maintained their separate identity. We know almost nothing about this sect of John the Baptist, except that it must have been quite widespread (see Acts 19:3). The only fast prescribed by the Old Testament was that of the Day of Atonement (Lev. 16:29). However, additional fasts were observed by the Pharisees twice a week, on Mondays and Thursdays. Great merit was placed on these fasts (see Lk. 18:12) and apparently the disciples of John imitated the Pharisees in this religious practice. Thus, while not commanded by the Law, these fasts were practised by the most devout and religious people among the Jews.

Jesus and his disciples ignored this custom, and the question was naturally raised, "Why are you not as religious as the Pharisees?" Jesus answered in a parabolic saying, "Can the wedding guests fast while the bridegroom is with them? As long as they have the bridegroom with them, they cannot fast" (Mk. 2:19). In the symbolic language of the East, the wedding is a symbol of the day of salvation (see Rev. 19:7). While Jesus is with his disciples, he has brought the gifts and fellowship of the Kingdom of God. Wedding songs resound. There is no place for mourning. This is the time for the bridal festivities; why should my disciples fast? However, this joy is to be strangely interrupted; "The days will come, when the bridegroom is taken away from them, and then they will fast in that day" (Mk. 2:20). The root of the verb, "taken away", is used twice in the Greek translation of Isaiah 53:8. "In humiliation his judgment was taken away . . . Because his life is taken from the earth for the transgressions of my people he was brought into death." Jesus is referring to the fact that he is to suffer the fate of the Suffering Servant: a violent death.

On one occasion, James and John came to Jesus with a request for places of honour in his coming kingdom. Jesus answered, "You do not know what you are asking. Are you able to drink the cup that I drink or to be baptised with the baptism with which I am baptised?" (Mk. 10:38). The cup is clearly the bitter cup of suffering, and the baptism is the overwhelming experiences of agony and death that await him.

The same idea of being overwhelmed in death appears in a saying in Luke 12:50. "I have a baptism to be baptised with; and how I am constrained until it is accomplished." Such a saying indicates not only that Jesus is conscious that death awaits him; it suggests more than this—that somehow his death is the goal of his mission.

The clearest statement in the Synoptics of this mission of death is found in Mark 10:45: "For the Son of man came not to be served but to serve, and to give his life a ransom for many." This pictures the lives of the many as being forfeited because of sin, and Jesus claims to be able to redeem them by giving his own life.

One of the most important intimations of his death is found in the institution of the Last Supper, which became the Lord's Supper in the early church. Mark relates that as they were eating, Jesus took bread, and blessed, and broke it, and gave it to them saying, "Take; this is my body." And he took a cup and when he had given thanks, he gave it to them, and they all drank of it. And Jesus said, "This is my blood of the covenant, which is poured out for many" (Mk. 14:22-24). Matthew adds the phrase, "for the forgiveness of sins" (Mt. 26:28).

Background for this teaching about the covenant, which certainly can be nothing but a new covenant, is found in the covenant of Sinai and the covenant of forgiveness. When Moses received the law from the hand of God he took the blood of burnt offerings and peace offerings and threw half of it against the altar. After reading to the people the covenant and securing from them the promise of obedience, he threw the other half of the blood upon the people saying, "Behold the blood of the covenant which the Lord has made with you in accordance with all these words" (Exod. 24:8). This old covenant is connected with sacrifice but there is no mention of the forgiveness of sins.

The new covenant is specifically a covenant of forgiveness. God promised through Jeremiah a new covenant when he would write his law upon the hearts of the people and would enter into a new intimacy of relationship with them because he would forgive their iniquity and remember their sin no more (Jer. 31:34). In the symbolism of the cup, Jesus in effect asserts the fulfilment of this new covenant whose objective is the forgiveness of sins. Furthermore this new covenant can be inaugurated only on the basis of sacrifice — not now the sacrifice of bulls or goats but the sacrifice of Jesus' broken body and shed blood.

While Jesus is represented as viewing his death as the goal

of his mission, death is not the end. Once the disciples have become convinced of Jesus' messiahship, even though he is not filling the role of Messiah as traditionally understood, Mark, followed by Matthew and Luke, records that, "He began to teach them that the Son of Man must suffer many things and be rejected by the elders and the chief priests and the scribes and be killed, and after three days rise again" (Mk. 8:31; cf. Mt. 16:21, Lk. 9:22). This was an utterly shocking statement. According to Daniel and the Jewish apocalypse of Enoch, the Son of Man was a heavenly supernatural figure who would come from heaven with power and glory to establish God's eternal Kingdom on earth. When Jesus spoke of the coming of the Son of Man in the glory of his Father with the holy angels (Mk. 8:38), this made sense to the disciples. But it threw them into confusion at two points: the Son of Man was a heavenly supernatural figure; Jesus was a man among men. How could this humble Jesus be the heavenly Son of Man? And furthermore, if Jesus was either Messiah or Son of Man, how could he suffer and die? It was the role of the Davidic King to *destroy* his enemies with the breath of his lips; how could he be delivered up to be put to death? It was the role of the heavenly Son of Man to come to earth with the glory of the Father to establish God's rule on the earth. How could he be killed? This prediction must have cast the disciples into utter bewilderment. We must remember this important fact. The Jews did not understand Isaiah 53 to have anything to do with the Messiah. As a matter of fact, in its own context, it is not a prophecy of Messiah but of an unnamed servant of the Lord (Isa. 52:13). By Old Testament definition, Messiah—Davidic king—was to destroy his enemies. By definition, the Son of Man was to reign in God's Kingdom. But rejection, death—this was unheard of. No wonder Peter rebuked Jesus for this saying. But Jesus affirmed that it was his destiny to die—and to rise again. He gives no explanation of his resurrection; he merely affirms it.[2]

This prediction about his resurrection is twice repeated. After the transfiguration, "he charged them to tell no one what they had seen, until the Son of man should have risen from the dead" (Mk. 9:9; cf. Mt. 17:9). At the moment, let it suffice to point out that there is no reference in the Old Testament or in Jewish literature that the *Son of Man* should rise from the dead. Apparently, Jesus did not explain at any length what this meant, for Mark adds, "So they kept the matter to themselves, questioning what the rising from the dead meant" (Mk. 9:10). The force of this fact will be enlarged on later.

Shortly thereafter, Mark relates that Jesus was journeying through Galilee. Jesus did not engage in public ministry but was teaching his disciples. "The Son of man will be delivered into the hands of men, and they will kill him; and when he is killed, after three days he will rise" (Mk. 9:31; cf. Mt. 17:22-23). However, the disciples did not understand the saying, and they were afraid to ask him.

Mark relates a further prediction of Jesus' sufferings and resurrection on the final journey to Jerusalem. "Behold, we are going up to Jerusalem; and the Son of Man will be delivered to the chief priests and the scribes, and they will condemn him to death, and deliver him to the Gentiles; and they will mock him, and spit upon him, and scourge him, and kill him; and after three days he will rise" (Mk. 19:33-34). Again there is no explanation or elaboration, but merely the affirmation that he would rise from the dead.

A final prediction is placed immediately after the Last Supper. Jesus said, "You will all fall away; for it is written, 'I will strike the shepherd, and the sheep will be scattered.' But after I am raised up, I will go before you to Galilee" (Mk. 14:27-28; cf. Mt. 26:31-32).

The Gospel of John bears witness to Jesus' conviction that he must die and rise again, but in very different terms from the Synoptics. When certain Greeks came to Philip asking to see Jesus, Jesus said, "Unless a grain of wheat falls into the ground and dies, it remains alone; but if it dies, it bears much fruit" (Jn. 12:24). Here, in a metaphor, Jesus is made to predict his own death, but beyond death is a new emergence into life to bear much fruit.

In the parable of the Good Shepherd, Jesus said, "I am the good shepherd. The good shepherd lays down his life for the sheep . . . I lay down my life, that I may take it again. No one takes it from me, but I lay it down of my own accord. I have power to lay it down and I have power to take it again" (Jn. 10:11, 18). The construction in the second sentence is a construction of purpose. "I lay down my life, *in order that* I may take it again." This indicates that the resurrection is not a mere event following Jesus' death, but the essential completion of his death. Resurrection is the purpose of his death.

In the Fourth Gospel, Jesus several times speaks of his death as a "lifting up", a "being glorified". And as Moses lifted up the serpent in the wilderness, so must the Son of Man be lifted up" (Jn. 3:14). "When you have lifted up the Son of Man, then you will know that I am he, and that I do nothing of my own authority but speak thus as the Father taught me" (Jn. 8:28). "And I, when I am lifted up from the earth, will draw all men to myself" (Jn. 12:32). His uplifting is also his glorification. "The hour has come for the Son of Man to be glorified" (Jn. 12:23). "Now is the Son of Man glorified, and in him God is glorified" (Jn. 13:31). His death will not be a mere human tragedy, but will be the means by which he will return to the glory from which he had come. "Now, Father, glorify me in thy own presence with the glory which I had with thee before the world was made" (Jn. 17:5).

A reflection of his suffering is seen in another saying about the bread of life. Jesus asserts that he is the bread of life which came down from heaven (Jn. 6:33-35), that as the Son of Man he gives the food which endures unto eternal life (Jn. 6:27), that men must eat the flesh and drink the blood of the Son of Man to experience this life (Jn. 6:5), and that the bread which he will give them is his flesh (Jn. 6:51). "These passages show conclusively that a reference to the death of Jesus is intended — he will give his flesh in death — and suggest a sacrificial meaning."[3]

A moment's reflection will prove that the sayings about death and resurrection in the Synoptics and in John represent two independent traditions. Matthew and Luke follow Mark, quoting his predictions of Jesus' death practically verbatim. John reports with equal clarity that Jesus foresaw his death. In fact, John brings out aspects of Jesus' death which are not found in the Synoptics. It is the hour of Jesus' glorification. John records predictions of both death and resurrection but in very different idiom. Thus we have two independent witnesses to the fact that the goal of Jesus' mission was death and resurrection.

Thus far we have surveyed the Gospel evidence with only one purpose in mind: to discover the importance of the resurrection in the thought of the early church. The Gospels are records of what the early church believed about Jesus. It believed that he was conscious that it was his mission to die, but beyond death lay resurrection. It believed that he had clearly predicted both his death and resurrection. We must now ask the question, Does the Gospel tradition accurately reflect the mind of Jesus? Or does it reflect only what the early church believed about Jesus?

We live in a day when many "advanced" scholars are committed to a method of studying the New Testament called Form Criticism (*Formgeschichte*). Form Criticism is the study of the Gospel tradition while it was known only in oral form. Mark was written about A.D. 60, Matthew and Luke possibly a little later. This means that for a period of some thirty years, the traditions about the words and deeds of Jesus were not written down but were handed down by word of mouth, being preserved in oral form. This is an established fact. Thus the study of the oral tradition is a legitimate method.[4] However, in its extreme form, form critics hold that the early church radically transformed the oral tradition, putting into the mouth of Jesus out of reverence for him many words that he did not say. Thus the Gospels are a record of the faith of the church but not of the historical Jesus. So, many form critics maintain that Jesus' predictions of his death and resurrection are reflections of Christian faith, not accurate historical reports.

This position is faced with a problem of explaining how these sayings arose. It is not simply that Jesus predicted his death and resurrection; it is as the *Son of Man* that he is to die and rise again. This is true both in the Synoptics and in John. We will discuss in a later chapter the background of the Son of Man. The Son of Man was a heavenly, supernatural being who comes to God to receive the Kingdom of God, and then rules forever in that Kingdom over all the nations on earth. *The Son of Man is not a suffering and dying figure;* he is a heavenly glorious figure whose destiny is not to die but to reign. Furthermore, the early church never used the terms "Son of Man" to designate Jesus. The term is never found in Paul or the other New Testament epistles. It is used in Revelation 1 : 13

to refer to the glorified Christ, and in Acts 7: 56 of the heavenly Jesus receiving the soul of the martyr Stephen. Furthermore, "Son of Man" is never a term used by men to designate Jesus in his earthly ministry. *It is a term used only by Jesus to designate himself;* and the idea that it is as the Son of Man that he must suffer and die and rise again is so novel that *it can only have arisen in the mind of Jesus.* It seems to the present author that, entirely apart from any dogmatic considerations about the deity of Christ, we stand on solid critical ground in maintaining that at this point the Gospels accurately reflect the mind of Jesus. His death and resurrection were of supreme importance both for the early church and for Jesus himself.

At this point, a difficulty arises. If Jesus predicted his own resurrection, were not these predictions enough to account for the rise of the resurrection faith? If Jesus had tried to prepare his disciples for his violent death, must we not picture them as remembering that he had also predicted his resurrection? Would not these predictions create in them the hope of resurrection so that the resurrection appearances were a result of an antecedent belief in resurrection?

On the contrary, the Gospels represent the disciples as being unprepared for Jesus' death and overwhelmed by it. Mark (14: 50), followed by Matthew (26: 56), relates that when Jesus was seized by the soldiers, all the disciples forsook him and fled. Peter is made, out of fear, to deny that he had been a disciple of Jesus (Mk. 14: 66-72). In the Synoptic Gospels, the only friends of Jesus who were present with him in his last moments were a few women (Mk. 15: 40-41); the disciples, by name, drop completely out of the picture. Luke alone (23: 49) records that Jesus' friends stood at a distance watching the crucifixion. Probably Luke means to designate his disciples. John alone (19: 26) mentions that "the disciple whom he loved" stood near the cross with his mother.

On Easter Sunday, John reports that the disciples were gathered together in a closed room "for fear of the Jews" (Jn. 20: 19). Luke records the feeling of discouragement of two disciples going to Emmaus: "But we had hoped that he was the one to redeem Israel" (Lk. 24: 21). This hope was a thing of the past: we *had* hoped (the Greek is an imperfect). Jesus was dead; and with him died their hopes.

The Gospels represent the disciples as being utterly unprepared for Jesus' death. It came as an unexpected event, and it left them in a state of emotional shock. Does this fact not contradict the witness of the Gospels that Jesus had on several occasions alluded to his death and on at least three occasions had specifically predicted his rejection, death, and subsequent resurrection?

This apparent contradiction in the Gospel data can be resolved when we place ourselves in the actual historical situation of the disciples. We will survey in a later chapter the Old Testament view of the Messiah, and the contemporary Jewish hopes. *Nowhere do we find the expectation of a Messiah whose fate is to suffer and die.* In fact, suffering and death seemed to be a flat contradiction of the Old Testament messianic hopes. The Messiah was to be either a divinely endowed Davidic King, or a heavenly Son of Man; and in either case, it was his destiny *to reign in God's Kingdom.*

The Triumphal Entry is significant at this point. Jesus entered Jerusalem in deliberate fulfilment of the prophecy in Zechariah 9: 9, which embodied a claim to messiahship but not one which matched any of the current expectations. The manner of his entry revealed his messianic dignity to those who were able and inclined to understand, but concealed it from others. The people recognised the messianic claims and cried, "Blessed be he who comes in the name of the Lord! Blessed be the kingdom of our father David that is coming" (Mk. 11: 9-10). However, in the Markan account, the people do not hail him as Messiah; but Matthew understands this to be their meaning. He has the people hail "the Son of David" (Mt. 21:9), which is a term synonymous with Messiah. However, neither the priests nor the Roman governor, Pilate, take any steps to suppress a messianic movement. The situation is accurately described in the words of our finest contemporary commentator on Mark, Vincent Taylor:

> The atmosphere is one of dangerous tensions, but the tension breaks and dies away . . . Jesus must have observed the growing messianic tension among His disciples and have realised that His teaching about a suffering messiah had failed . . . By previous arrangement He sends two disciples

for the colt, intending to fulfil Zechariah's prophecy. Unable to deny that He is the promised messiah, He seeks to show to His disciples and to the crowd the kind of messiah He is, no man of war, but lowly and riding upon an ass. The crowd is puzzled, but penetrates His meaning to see that He is not to be the messiah of their hopes. That is why they turned against Him.[5]

This is also why his disciples forsook him when he was taken captive. Their minds were so completely imbued with the idea of a conquering Messiah whose role it was to subdue his enemies that when they saw him broken and bleeding under the scourging, a helpless prisoner in the hands of Pilate, and when they saw him led away, nailed to a cross to die as a common criminal, all their messianic hopes for Jesus were shattered. It is a sound psychological fact that we hear only what we are prepared to hear. Jesus' predictions of his suffering and death fell on deaf ears. The disciples, in spite of his warnings, were unprepared for it, and equally unprepared for his resurrection. We are on firm ground, therefore, when we conclude that the Gospels are accurate when they represent Jesus as anticipating his own death and resurrection, even though his predictions utterly failed to prepare them for the events which actually occurred. This tentative conclusion will be confirmed when we make a detailed study of the contemporary Jewish messianic hopes.

It is clear, then, that the early church as represented by our Gospels believed that Jesus viewed his ministry as culminating in his death and resurrection; and we find good reason to conclude that the Gospels accurately represent the mind of Jesus himself. However, the fact that Jesus both foresaw and predicted His resurrection *does not account for the resurrection faith of the early church*. The disciples did not understand Jesus' meaning. They were utterly dismayed and confused by his death, and were not expecting his resurrection. Something had to happen to create in them that faith—that Jesus was alive.

When we turn to the book of Acts and its account of the early church, we find that the central message of the earliest Christians was the resurrection of Christ. Acts records several sermons in the early chapters, but many critics have maintained that Acts is not a historically reliable document. It may be used as a source for Christian faith at the time when it was written—late, we are told, in the first century. However, equally competent scholars find critical reasons for accepting the essential historical trustworthiness of Acts,[6] and we follow their lead.

On the day of Pentecost, Peter preached the first Christian sermon, explaining what was the meaning of the pentecostal experience. His message is simple. The Jews have crucified Jesus. God has raised him from the dead and exalted him to heaven and seated him at God's own right hand. The risen and exalted Lord has given his people the Holy Spirit (Acts 2: 14-36). *Everything depends on the fact of Jesus' resurrection.* Peter refers only obliquely to Jesus' life; he was a man "attested to you by God with mighty works and wonders and signs which God did through him in your midst" (Acts 2: 22). No reference is made to Jesus' teaching about the coming of God's Kingdom. Peter's central message is that because God has raised Jesus from the dead and exalted him at his right hand, he has "made him both Lord and Christ, this Jesus whom you crucified" (Acts 2: 36). "Christ" is the Greek equivalent of Messiah— messianic king. Peter does not mean to say that Jesus *became* Messiah at his resurrection-exaltation, for it was as Messiah that he suffered (Acts 3: 18). However, by virtue of his resurrection-ascension, he has entered into a new stage of his messianic reign. He has begun to reign as messianic king.

In his second sermon after the healing of the lame man at the Beautiful Gate, the same theme of death-resurrection-ascension is the central message. "God raised [him] from the dead. To this we are witnesses" (Acts 3: 15).

The first opposition experienced by the earliest Christians came from the Sadducees because they were "proclaiming in Jesus the resurrection from the dead" (Acts 4: 3). We know both from the New Testament (Acts 23: 8) and from extra-biblical sources that the Sadducees did not believe in any form of resurrection, while the Pharisees did believe in a resurrection at the last day. The Sadducees tolerated the Pharisees and did not trouble them for their faith in resurrection. Why then should they trouble the Christians for their proclamation? Because the Christians preached *in Jesus* the resurrection from the dead. This took the resurrection out of the realm of theological speculation and made it a fact of historical affirmation. The Sadducees could debate with the Pharisees about whether there would be an eschatological resurrection; but if the Christians were right, there could be no debate with the facts of history; the Sadducees were proven wrong.

The important point at the moment is that the resurrection of Jesus was the central proclamation of the early church.

All this is supported by the choice of Matthias as an apostle to take the place of Judas. The qualification for this position was that one must have been a companion of Jesus and his disciples, and the primary ministry of the twelve was to "become . . . a witness to his resurrection" (Acts 1: 22). It is clear that not the life of Jesus, not his teachings, not even his sacrificial death, was the central emphasis in the earliest Christian proclamation; it was the resurrection of Christ.

That the resurrection continued to be central in early Christian proclamation is shown by reports of later sermons. When the Gospel was taken for the first time to Gentiles, Peter proclaimed to Cornelius a very brief statement about the life and death of Jesus. Then he affirmed: "God raised him on the third day and made him manifest; not to all the people but to us who were chosen by God as witnesses, who ate and drank with him after he rose from the dead" (Acts 10: 40-41). Peter witnessed not only to the resurrection but to his own experience of renewed fellowship with the risen Lord.

Luke obviously does not record all the sermons preached in the early years of the church. Rather, he gives samples of preaching illustrating the expanding ministry of the church. He gives a summary of one of Paul's first sermons in his first missionary journey in the Gentile world in Antioch of Pisidia. First, Paul recalls some of the highlights of redemptive history from The Exodus to Jesus. He dwells on the rejection of Jesus by the Jewish leaders, leading to Jesus' crucifixion. He says nothing about the saving efficacy of Jesus' death, merely the fact of his execution. Then he dwells on the resurrection, seeing it as a fulfilment of the second Psalm: "Thou art my Son, today I have begotten thee." Paul's proclamation of salvation (Acts 13: 26) and forgiveness of sins (Acts 13: 38) seems to be based altogether on the resurrection of Jesus from the dead.

The centrality of the resurrection is again illustrated by Paul's sermon on Mars Hill in Athens. There he encountered certain Epicurean and Stoic philosophers (Acts 17: 18). The Epicureans' chief aim was to relieve life of all fear, especially the fear of death. They recognised that the gods exist but felt they had no interest in human affairs. They held an atomic theory of matter, including the human soul. The soul is dissolved at death into the atoms which compose it and has no future existence to dread or to desire.

The Stoics were materialistic monists, believing that the deity was a fine invisible fiery vapour which interpenetrated all things. At death, the soul was reabsorbed by the world-soul — the divine fiery essence of which individual souls were sparks. Thus neither Epicureans nor Stoics believed in personal immortality, as did the Platonic philosophers.

Nevertheless, the climax of Paul's sermon was Jesus and the resurrection (Acts 17: 18). He proclaimed a day of judgment of which God has given a pledge and token by raising Jesus from the dead (Acts 17: 31). Some people believe that Paul failed in Athens because he did not preach the cross (1 Cor. 2: 2); he is said to have compromised his message by trying to be a philosopher to the philosophers. This is not true. No message could have been more antithetical to Athenian beliefs than the proclamation of Jesus' resurrection. Such an idea was utterly alien to the thinking of both Epicureans and Stoics; yet Paul proclaims an impossible (to them) truth. The whole Gospel is encapsulated in the proclamation of the resurrection of Jesus.

It is a commonplace in biblical studies that Paul in his extant correspondence says very little about the life and teaching of Jesus. The entire Pauline message is the explication of the meaning of the death and resurrection-exaltation of Jesus. To Paul, Jesus is not primarily a human teacher of wisdom or preacher of divine truths; he is the incarnate Son of God who died an atoning death, was raised by the power of God from the dead and exalted to become Lord over all (Phil. 2: 5-11). The primacy of Jesus' resurrection is clearly affirmed in the introduction to the Roman epistle. Jesus was "descended from David according to the flesh and designated

Son of God in power according to the Spirit of holiness by his resurrection from the dead" (Rom. 1: 3-4). "According to the flesh" is a common Greek idiom meaning "on the human level". The word rendered *declared* Son of God means "appointed". Paul means not that Jesus *became* the Son of God by the resurrection in an adoptionistic sense, but that he who during his earthly ministry was the Son of God in weakness and power became by the resurrection the Son of God *in power*.[7] "For to this end Christ died and lived again, that he might be Lord both of the dead and of the living" (Rom. 14: 9). The resurrection is confirmation of Jesus' divine sonship; it means entrance into his supreme ministry of lordship. Paul's entire message rests upon the factuality of the resurrection of Christ.

For the author of Hebrews, the important thing is the exaltation of Christ, which depends upon his resurrection. "When he has made purification for sins, he sat down at the right hand of the Majesty on high" (Heb. 1: 3). Christ is the living High Priest who continues his ministry of intercession in the heavenly temple (Heb. 7: 25). The whole message of Hebrews depends on the reality of the resurrection of Christ.

The same is true of the Revelation. Jesus is the one who died and yet is alive for evermore, who has the keys of Death and Hades (Rev. 1: 18). The portrait of Jesus in Revelation 1: 12-16 is that of the living, exalted, glorified Lord—a picture which is nothing but a fancy of the imagination unless Christ is actually raised from the dead.

This survey has made it clear that the resurrection of Jesus is no incidental or peripheral matter. It is not merely a question of the integrity and historical trustworthiness of a few resurrection stories. The entire New Testament was written from the perspective of the resurrection. Indeed, the resurrection may be called the major premise of the early Christian faith.

The early Christians believed that Jesus foresaw both his death and his resurrection. The Gospels were written not to record the words and deeds of a great teacher. They were written because their authors believed that the Jesus whom they had known could not be conquered by death but was still alive. They believed that the real mission of Jesus could be understood only when viewed through the eyes of the resurrection faith. According to Acts, the resurrection was the primary message of the earliest Christians. It is the basic presupposition of the New Testament epistles. The cornerstone of the entire New Testament is the resurrection.

If this faith is not founded on fact, the message of the entire New Testament rests on a fallacy.

NOTES

1. C. F. Evans, *Resurrection and the New Testament* (Naperville: Allenson, 1920), p. 1.
2. V. Taylor, *The Gospel according to Mark* (London: Macmillan, 1952), p. 295.
3. C. K. Barrett, *The Gospel according to St. John* (London: S.P.C.K., 1955), p. 246.
4. See G. E. Ladd, *The New Testament and Criticism* (London and Grand Rapids: Hodder and Stoughton, and Eerdmans, 1967), ch. VI.
5. V. Taylor, *op. cit.*, p. 452.
6. See F. F. Bruce, *The Speeches in Acts* (London: Inter-Varsity, 1943); H. N. Ridderbos, *The Speeches of Peter in the Acts of the Apostles* (London: Tyndale, 1961); I. H. Marshall, "The Resurrection in the Acts of the Apostles," *Apostolic History and the Gospel*, ed. by W. W. Gasque and R. P. Martin (London: Paternoster, 1970), pp. 92–107.
7. See F. F. Bruce, *The Epistle of Paul to the Romans* (Grand Rapids: Eerdmans, 1963) ;p. 72.

CHAPTER 4

Resurrection in the Old Testament

WE MUST SURVEY the Old Testament teaching on resurrection to discover if it throws any light upon the belief in the resurrection of Jesus. Is the Old Testament so full of the hope of the resurrection that the disciples applied this idea to Jesus once they came to believe that he was the Messiah?

To understand the Old Testament hope, we must first of all understand the Old Testament concept of man. It stands in sharp contrast to the Greek view of man. One of the most influential Greek concepts of man stems from Platonic thought and has often had a strong influence on Christian theology. It is that man is a dualism of body and soul. The soul belongs to the real, permanent, noumenal world; the body belongs to the visible, transitory, temporal, phenomenal world.[1] The body is not thought to be *ipso facto* evil, as was the case in later Gnostic thought, but it is a hindrance to the cultivation of the mind and the soul. The wise man is he who learns how to discipline the body so that it is held in control and does not impair the cultivation of the soul. In this view, the soul is immortal, and "salvation" means the flight of the soul at death to escape the burden of the phenomenal world and find fulfilment in the world of eternal reality.

A verse in Paul, taken out of context, can be interpreted in this light. "We look not to the things that are seen but to the things that are unseen; for the things that are seen are transient, but the things that are unseen are eternal" (2 Cor. 4: 18). This sounds like Platonic dualism; but in the context of Pauline thought, the eternal "things that are not seen" means the world of God which eventually will break into this world and transform it.[2] This includes the resurrection of the body. Paul never conceives of the salvation of the soul apart from the body. Salvation means the redemption of the body and of the whole created order as well (Rom. 8: 21-23).

Paul's view is based upon the Old Testament view of man, in which man's "soul" (*nephesh*) is primarily his vitality, his life—never a separate "part" of man. "Spirit" is first of all God's spirit (*ruach*), his breath, his power (Isa. 31: 3; 40: 7) which created and sustains all living things (Ps. 33: 6; 104: 29-30). God's spirit creates the human spirit (Zech. 12: 1), but neither man's soul nor spirit is viewed as an immortal part of man which survives death. Man's death occurs when his spirit—his breath—is withdrawn (Ps. 104: 29; Ecc. 12: 7), and his soul—his *nephesh*—may be said to die (Num. 23: 10, literally, "let my soul die the death of the righteous"; Jud. 16: 30, "let my soul die with the Philistines"). In other places, the soul (*nephesh*) is said to depart to Sheol (Ps. 16: 10, "For thou dost not give up my soul to Sheol"; cf. Ps. 30: 3; 94: 17). In these last references, *nephesh* is practically synonymous with the personal pronoun; there is no thought of an immortal soul existing after death. In sum, the Old Testament view of man is that he is an animated body rather than an incarnated soul.[3] "Life" in the Old Testament is bodily existence in this world in fellowship with the living God (Deut. 30: 15-20). Death means the end of *life* but not the cessation of *existence*. The dead exist in Sheol as "shades" (Prov. 9: 18; Isa. 14: 9; 26: 19). A "shade" is not man's soul or spirit; it is man himself, or rather a pale replica of a man. It is man stripped of his vitality and energy—a shadow of his earthly self. The evil thing about Sheol is that in death, man is cut off from fellowship with God (Ps. 6: 5; 88: 10-12; 115: 17).

However, this is not the last word. The conviction grew that if God's people had truly enjoyed fellowship with God, even death could not disrupt that relationship. God is Lord both of the earth and of Sheol. "Whither shall I go from thy Spirit? Or whither shall I flee from thy presence? If I ascend to heaven, thou art there! If I make my bed in Sheol, thou art there!" (Ps. 139: 8).

Under this conviction, several of the Psalms express the

conviction of blessedness after death instead of the gloom of
the nether world. An important passage is Psalms 16: 9-11:

> Therefore my heart is glad, and my soul rejoices;
>   my body also dwells secure.
> For thou dost not give me [lit. my soul] up to Sheol,
>   or let thy godly one see the Pit.
> Thou dost show me the path of life;
>   in thy presence there is fulness of joy,
>   in thy right hand are pleasures for evermore.

Some interpreters understand this to mean only that God will
preserve his saint from dying. However, there is no hint of
danger or sickness in the context. "He is cherishing the hope
that in this life and beyond he may find in God his portion
still, and so may be delivered from Sheol."[4] "The real question
in Ps. XVI is that of communion with the Living God; the
writer foresees no end to this; he does not understand how its
persistence will be possible, but that does not trouble his mind,
because it depends on God."[5] The important thing to note is
that survival after death is not a characteristic inherent in man;
it rests altogether with God.

A second passage is Psalms 49: 15:

> But God will ransom my soul from the power of Sheol,
>   for he will receive me.

A recent commentator thinks that this passage means that the
author expects to experience an assumption similar to that of
Enoch and Elijah.[6] However, it seems more likely that this
should be understood as expressing a conviction similar to that
of Psalms 16.

> In death itself the difference between the man who serves
> God and the man who scorns Him is made apparent. The
> psalmist is sure that his God will not let him suffer the fate
> of the impious; through faith, he asserts that God will be
> with him, the hand of Sheol is impotent against the presence
> of Yahweh with those who are His own.[7]

The same thought is probably expressed in Psalms 73: 24:

> Thou dost guide me with thy counsel,
>   and afterward thou wilt receive me to glory.

There is some difficulty with the text, but Rowley's conclusion seems sound: the Psalmist "first declares that he enjoys God's fellowship here and now, and if God is to receive him, it must be to future fellowship . . . Both before death and after death he has a secure treasure in the fellowship of God."[8]

Such passages give us only glimpses of a hope of a blessed existence after death. It is important to note that the hope is based on confidence in God's power over death, not on a view of something immortal in man. The Psalmists do not reflect on what *part* of man survives death—his soul or spirit; nor is there any reflection on the nature of the after life. There is merely the confidence that even death cannot destroy the reality of fellowship with the living God. This is very different from the Greek view of immortality. "The psalmists . . . cannot conceive that this communion [with God] can ever be broken even by death."[9]

There also gradually emerged in the Old Testament the hope of bodily resurrection. That the Hebrews believed that death need not be the end of human existence is proved by the bodily translation of Enoch and Elijah. Furthermore, there are stories of resurrections wrought by Elijah and Elisha (1 Kgs. 17: 17-24; 2 Kgs. 4: 31-37; 13: 21). However, these are all exceptional cases and lead to no conclusions about resurrection in general.

In the prophets, we find several clear intimations of the hope of resurrection. The first is in Hosea 6: 1-2:

> Come, let us return to the LORD;
>   for he has torn, that he may heal us;
>   he has stricken, and he will bind us up.
> After two days he will revive us;
>   on the third day he will raise us up,
>   that we may live before him.

Some scholars see here a reference to individual resurrection, but the passage more likely refers to the restoration of the nation. God has punished Israel for her apostasy. Here is expressed a plea to return to the Lord to receive healing; and if Israel turns, in a very short time God will restore the nation to its favoured position as his people.

The same idea is found in Ezekiel 37, where Ezekiel has a vision of a valley of dry bones which came together and then were covered with flesh. This clearly refers to the resurrection of the nation (Ezek. 37: 11-13), not to individual resurrections. However, the very fact that the vision sees the restoration of dead bones to life suggests that the *idea* of bodily resurrection was familiar. "There is no doubt that the symbolism that [Ezekiel] employs raised among the Jews the question of renewal of life for the departed."[10]

The first clear reference to resurrection is found in Isaiah 25-26. In Isaiah 25: 8 we read, "He will swallow up death for ever, and the Lord God will wipe away tears from all faces." This verse appears in an eschatological context of the establishment of God's Kingdom on the earth and the gathering of his people to enjoy the blessings of his rule. It pictures an entirely new situation in which death is no more. This is not yet a promise of resurrection, but only of the abolition of death.

However, Isaiah 26: 19 expresses the confidence in resurrection:

Thy dead shall live, their bodies shall rise.
O dwellers in the dust, awake and sing for joy!

This does not appear to be a general resurrection, but only of God's people.[11]

A resurrection of both the righteous and the unrighteous is clearly affirmed in Daniel 12: 2: "And many of those who sleep in the dust of the earth shall awake, some to everlasting life, and some to shame and everlasting contempt." This may refer to a "general" resurrection,[12] that is, a resurrection of *all* men. On the other hand, the text affirms the resurrection of *many*, not of all, and the resurrection may be limited to Israelites.[13] The righteous are raised to "everlasting life". This is the first occurrence of this phrase in the Bible. The Hebrew has "to the life of the age", i.e., to a life that extends indefinitely into the future. By New Testament times, the equivalent Greek phrase meant "the life of the Age to Come" (see Mk. 10: 30). In Daniel it clearly refers to an eschatological resurrection of the body. Rowley thinks that "what is in mind is physical life in this world, side by side with those who had not passed through death."[14] This depends altogether on how one understands the word "physical". It cannot designate a body exactly like the physical body of this age, for this body is shut up to death, and the resurrection body transcends this limitation.

We have completed our survey of the idea of the afterlife and of the resurrection in the Old Testament. We have discovered that the Old Testament does not consider the soul of man to be an immortal part of him. On the other hand, death does not end existence; the dead exist in the shadowy realm of Sheol. Gradually, the conviction emerges that even death cannot separate God's people from enjoyment of fellowship with God, and this leads finally to the belief in the eschatological destruction of death and the resurrection of the body. This was a logical outcome of the Old Testament view of man, for whom bodily existence is essential to the full meaning of life. The idea of man as an animated body, and the faith in a sovereign God whose power and promises could not be broken by death, led to the belief in the eschatological resurrection of the body.

However, this belief *is* eschatological. It is resurrection on the last day. It provides no help in explaining the rise of belief in Jesus' resurrection. Therefore we must pursue our search a step further. What was the belief in resurrection in Jesus' day? Beyond that we must ask, What was the Old Testament expectation about the coming of Messiah? Does the Old Testament predict the sufferings, death and resurrection of Messiah? Can we not account for the rise of the resurrection faith in terms of Old Testament promise?

This question is particularly relevant because the New Testament seems to say that all that happened to Jesus was clearly predicted in the prophets. Jesus said to the two men on the Emmaus road:

"O foolish men, and slow of heart to believe all that the

prophets have spoken! Was it not necessary that the Christ should suffer these things and enter into his glory?" And beginning with Moses and all the prophets, he interpreted to them in all the scriptures the things concerning himself (Lk. 24: 25-27).

Again, Paul writes, "Christ died for our sins in accordance with the scriptures, . . . he was buried, . . . he was raised on the third day in accordance with the scriptures" (1 Cor. 15: 3-4). We will discuss this problem later.

Our next question must be: How did the idea of resurrection develop in post-Old Testament times? What were the ideas of resurrection which developed in the Judaism contemporary with Jesus? Possibly Judaism developed ideas of resurrection which will help explain the rise of the belief in Jesus' resurrection.

NOTES

1. This view is spelled out in detail in the author's book, *The Pattern of New Testament Truth* (Grand Rapids: Eerdmans, 1968), chap. 1.
2. For this problem, see *ibid.*, p. 99.
3. See N. W. Porteus in *The Interpreter's Dictionary of the Bible*, K-Q, p. 243.
4. H. H. Rowley, *The Faith of Israel* (London: S.C.M., 1956), p. 174.
5. R. Martin-Achard, *From Death to Life* (Edinburgh: Oliver and Boyd, 1960), p. 153.
6. M. J. Dahood, *Psalms 1* (Garden City: Doubleday, 1966), p. 301.
7. Martin-Achard, *op. cit.*, p. 157. See also H. H. Rowley, *op. cit.*, p. 171, "Whereas the righteous may have suffering here, . . . hereafter he will have bliss, for God will take him to himself." See also G. von Rad, *Old Testament Theology* (New York: Harper, 1962), I, p. 406.
8. H. H. Rowley, *op. cit.*, p. 173.
9. Martin-Achard, *op. cit.*, p. 180.
10. *Ibid.*, p. 102.
11. G. von Rad, *op. cit.*, I, p. 407.
12. *Loc. cit.*
13. J. A. Montgomery, *The Book of Daniel* (New York: Scribners, 1927), p. 471.
14. H. H. Rowley, *op. cit.*, p. 168.

CHAPTER 5

The Resurrection in Judaism

WE POSSESS a fairly extensive literature from New Testament times which reflects to us contemporary Jewish ideas about many things, including the fate of the dead, resurrection, and the mission of Messiah. This literature may be described in three different groups. First is the Jewish intertestamental literature, usually referred to as the Apocrypha and Pseudepigrapha.[1] "Apocrypha" means "things that are hidden", and it is not clear how the term came to be used to designate a certain collection of books. The books of the Apocrypha are those books contained in the Roman Catholic Bible which the Protestant churches do not recognise as canonical. "Pseudepigrapha" means "false writings" in the sense that a given book is attributed to someone who obviously did not write it, e.g., Enoch, Baruch, Moses, etc. However, these are artificial designations which have arisen through historical accidents. It is more accurate to describe all of these books as Jewish apocryphal or intertestamental writings. The various books were produced by various groups within Judaism and reflect great diversity of viewpoints.

A second group of literature is the so-called Qumran writings, produced by a separatist sect in the first two centuries B.C. The most important of these writings are the Manual of Discipline, the Damascus Document, the Hymns, the War Scroll, and the commentaries on certain Old Testament books. The Qumran writings reflect ideas which are different from those found in the other Jewish intertestamental writings.

A third source of intertestamental ideas is the Talmudic

writings, representing the thinking of the Pharisaic scribes whose teachings formed the mainstream of Jewish thought after the fall of Jerusalem. These writings must be used with caution, for they were compiled much later than New Testament times. However, since they embody the "traditions of the elders" (Mk. 7: 35) which were preserved in oral form in Jesus' day, they reflect one important strand in Jewish thinking. Josephus, the great Jewish historian who wrote in the first century A.D., says that the Pharisees teach "that every soul is imperishable, but that only those of the righteous pass into another body, while those of the wicked are, on the contrary, punished with eternal torment."[2] The Sadducees, on the other hand, "deny the continuance of the soul and the punishments and rewards of the world below."[3] A Talmudic writing, called Sanhedrin, says, "According to their teaching, souls perish together with bodies."[4] Scholars agree practically universally that Josephus means to say that the Pharisees believe in a resurrection of the body as taught in Daniel 12: 2, while the Sadducees deny resurrection, but he expresses his thought in idiom meaningful to Gentiles.

In this survey, one fact about the character of Judaism is of great importance. The church throughout its history has placed great emphasis upon "orthodoxy"—correct thought. This was not true of Judaism. Normative in Judaism was "orthopraxy"—correct practice. If a Jew obeyed the Law of Moses he was considered orthodox, even though he might have different theological ideas from the mainstream of Judaism. Thus we may expect to find great variety in intertestamental Judaism about the fate of the soul and the resurrection of the body.

One of the most interesting books of the Apocrypha is Ecclesiasticus, or the Wisdom of Jesus, the Son of Sirach. This is the only apocryphal book whose author is known. Jesus, the son of Sirach, was a Jewish scribe or wise man whose profession was the teaching of the Old Testament Law. About 180 B.C. this scribe committed to writing the wisdom that he had been accustomed to impart orally. Jesus had no concept either of a happy afterlife or of resurrection; he perpetuates the Old Testament idea of Sheol. It is a place devoid of pleasure (14: 16), a place of darkness (22: 11), a place of endless sleep

(46: 19), a place of silence (17: 27-28), a place of corruption (10: 11). Men cannot praise God in Sheol (or Hades). "From the dead, as from one who does not exist, thanksgiving has ceased" (18: 28). Death is a state of eternal rest (30: 17). "Do not forget; there is no coming back from death" (38: 21). The only immortality Sirach knows is a good name which can be remembered (39: 9; 41: 11-13; 44: 8) or the persistence of one's name in his children (11: 28; 46: 12). Thus, while Jesus ben Sirach lived and wrote before the emergence of the Pharisees and Sadducees, he holds a Sadducaic attitude towards death and the afterlife.

However, many other intertestamental writings express a belief in resurrection. One of the most vivid resurrection hopes is found in 2 Maccabees, a historical book written in the first century B.C. 2 Maccabees describes the persecution of the Jews by Antiochus Epiphanes in the second century B.C., many martyrdoms, and the hope of resurrection. This hope is expressed in numerous places.[5] The most vivid passage is the story of an elder by the name of Razis. Rather than fall into the hands of the hated Greeks, Razis took a sword and disembowelled himself. Then, standing on a steep rock, he tore out his bowels, and taking both his hands to them, he flung them at the crowds. So he died, "calling on Him who is lord of life and spirit to restore them to him again" (2 Macc. 14: 46). Here is the idea of bodily resurrection of the crudest physical sort.

A variant idea of resurrection is found in the Apocalypse of Baruch, a writing of the late first century A.D. The author of Baruch was overwhelmed by the tragedy of the destruction of Jerusalem. Reflecting on the evils of this life, he sees hope only in the world to come, including the resurrection of the righteous. Baruch asks in what form the righteous will be raised in the last day. He is told,

> The earth shall then assuredly restore the dead (which it now receives in order to preserve them). It shall make no change in their form, but as it has received so shall it preserve them, and as it delivered them unto it, so also shall it raise them. For then it will be necessary to show to the living that the dead have come to life again, and that those

who had departed have returned (again). And it shall come to pass, when they have severally recognised those whom they now know . . . then their splendour shall be glorified in changes, and the form of their face shall be turned into the light of their beauty that they may be able to acquire and receive the world which does not die, which is then promised to them . . . They shall . . . be transformed . . . into the splendour of angels . . . and time shall no longer age them. For in the heights of that world shall they dwell, and they shall be made like unto the angels, and be made equal to the stars, and they shall be changed into every form they desire, from beauty into loveliness and from light into splendour of glory (Apoc. Bar. 50: 2–51: 10).

Here is a twofold idea of resurrection. First, the dead are raised in precisely the same form in which they died that there may be mutual recognition. After that, they are transformed into the light and splendour of angels in order that they may dwell in the heights of the invisible heavenly world.

Another apocalypse, written at about the same time, is the Apocalypse of Ezra, usually designated 4 Ezra. This book, together with several additional chapters, is included in the Apocrypha under the name of 2 Esdras. However, the book is as apocalyptic and as pseudepigraphical as Baruch.

Ezra describes the coming of Messiah who will reign on earth in a temporary kingdom of four hundred years' duration. After this interim kingdom,

the earth shall give up those who are asleep in it, and the dust those who dwell silently in it; and the chambers shall give up the souls which have been committed to them. And the Most High shall be revealed upon the seat of judgment . . . Then the pit of torment shall appear, and opposite it shall be the place of rest; and the furnace of hell shall be disclosed, and opposite it the paradise of delight (4 Ez. 7: 32-36).

In another passage, Ezra speaks of the blessedness that awaits the righteous dead in the day of resurrection. "Their face is to shine like the sun, and . . . they are to be made like the light of the stars, being incorruptible from then on" (4 Ez. 7: 97).

One of the most interesting apocalyptic books is the book of Enoch, usually called 1 Enoch.[6] This book consists of five very diverse parts, whose history and compilation it is impossible to reconstruct. The several parts of Enoch were probably written during the first two centuries before Christ.

These five books contain very different eschatological expectations. The first book does not speak of a resurrection, but resurrection is implied. Enoch journeyed to the west where he visited Sheol, the intermediate state of the dead. Sheol is a place of four hollow places where the spirits of the dead reside. Of one group of sinful men, Enoch says that their spirits shall not be raised from Sheol, but shall be slain in the day of judgment (En. 22: 13). The statement that some of the wicked shall not be raised implies that the righteous will be raised, but resurrection is not spelled out in the first section of Enoch.

Resurrection is also implied in the fourth part of Enoch but is not spelled out (En. 90: 33). It is, however, only a resurrection of righteous Israelites.

The most interesting expectation of resurrection is found in the second part of Enoch, called the Similitudes, or Parables. It is a resurrection only of righteous Israelites, for the wicked "shall have no hope of rising from their beds, because they do not extol the name of the Lord of Spirits" (En. 46: 6). However, the righteous may expect to be raised from their grave.

> And in those days shall the earth also give back that which
>   has been entrusted to it,
> And Sheol also shall give back that which it has received,
> And hell shall give back that which it owes.
> For in those days the Elect One [the heavenly Son of Man]
>   shall arise,
> And he shall choose the righteous and holy from among
>   them [the dead];
> For the day has drawn nigh that they should be saved.
>   (En. 51: 1-2).

The nature of the resurrection is described in another passage.

> And the righteous and elect shall be saved on that day,
> And they shall never thenceforth see the face of the sinners
>   and unrighteous.
> And the Lord of Spirits will abide over them,
> And with that Son of Man shall they eat
> And lie down and rise up for ever and ever.
> And the righteous and elect shall have arisen from the earth,
> And ceased to be of downcast countenance.
> And they shall have been clothed with garments of glory,
> And they shall be garments of life from the Lord of Spirits;
> And your garments shall not grow old,
> Nor your glory pass away before the Lord of Spirits.
>   (En. 62: 13-16).

This concept of resurrection found in Jewish apocalyptic is very different from that of 2 Maccabees. The latter has a gross, physical idea of the resurrection, with all the natural organs preserved intact. The Apocalypse of Baruch sees a physical resurrection first, to be followed by a transformation of the body to become like angels. Enoch sees a bodily resurrection in some kind of transfigured body—"garments of glory". Neither of these authors expound what they mean by a transformed body.

A very different view of resurrection is found in the fifth book of 1 Enoch, if it is indeed to be described in terms of resurrection.

> And the righteous one shall arise from sleep,
> [Shall arise] and walk in the paths of righteousness,
> And all his path and conversation shall be in eternal goodness
>   and grace.
> He will be gracious to the righteous and give him eternal
>   uprightness,
> And He will give him power so that he shall be (endowed)
>   with goodness and righteousness,
> And he shall walk in eternal light
> And sin shall perish in darkness for ever,

And shall no more be seen from that day for evermore.
(1 En. 92: 3-5).

Be hopeful, for aforetime ye were put to shame through ill
and affliction; but now ye shall shine as lights of heaven, ye
shall shine and ye shall be seen, and the portals of heaven
shall be opened to you. (1 En. 104: 2).

Be hopeful, and cast not away your hope; for ye shall have
great joy as the angels of heaven. (1 En. 104: 4).

For ye shall become companions of the hosts of heaven.
(1 En. 104: 6).

However, in this part of Enoch we find a feature which is quite
uncommon in Judaism. It seems to be a resurrection not of the
body but of the spirit.

And the spirits of you who have died in righteousness shall
live and rejoice,
And their spirits shall not perish, nor their memorial from
before the face of the Great One
Unto all the generations of the world. (1 En. 103: 4).

Here we meet the idea of a blessed immortality of the spirit,
apparently without bodily resurrection, although it is described
in terms of resurrection. It is possible that the words about the
spirits of the righteous living and rejoicing is to be understood
in terms of the resurrection affirmed in 92: 3. In any case,
this "resurrection" is of a very transfigured sort in which the
redeemed have no more to do with earthly existence. The
portals of heaven are to be open to them, and they will become
companions of the hosts of heaven.

The Testaments of the Twelve Patriarchs is a book compiled
sometime in the first two centuries B.C.; but again, the history
of the book is impossible to reconstruct. Resurrection of
righteous Israelites is affirmed (Test. Judah 25: 1-4; Benjamin
10: 6-9; Zebulun 10: 4), but it does not add anything to our
study.

We must now ask if the sectarians of Qumran entertained an
idea of the resurrection. While this question is debated, the
answer seems to be that they were not much concerned about

the fate of the dead.[7] Some have attributed to them the idea of the immortality of the soul[8] — a view similar to that found in the fifth part of Enoch; but this is not at all clear.

A third group of Jewish writings is the Talmudic literature, a mass of material representing the thinking of the predominate school of Judaism which survived the fall of Jerusalem. We need here only say that resurrection of the body was a common doctrine in this literature. George Foot Moore, one of our foremost experts in this field, calls it "the primary eschatological doctrine of Judaism".[9]

Our survey of the Jewish literature of New Testament times reveals several facts. First, there was no uniformity in eschatological beliefs. The Sadducees, represented by Ecclesiasticus, had no place for resurrection. The fifth book of Enoch conceives of a resurrection of the spirit rather than of the body. The Qumranians seemed little interested in the question. Resurrection is most prominent in the apocalyptic literature and in the later Talmudic writings, and since we believe that the New Testament writings stand in the tradition of Jewish apocalyptic,[10] this fact is important for our purposes.

Second, the predominant eschatology of apocalyptic and Talmudic writings is the resurrection of the body. Sometimes this is described in gross physical terms, sometimes in terms of some sort of transformation of the body.

Third, this survey is of no help in providing background for the belief in Jesus' resurrection. The Jewish hope is an altogether eschatological hope — the resurrection of the righteous at the last day. Jesus' resurrection is an event which occurred in history, not at the end of history. There are, however, some striking analogies between certain apocalyptic ideas of the resurrection body and the New Testament portrayal of Jesus' resurrection body. This question will be discussed later.

There remains a final important question. Jesus was not merely a man; he was believed to be the Messiah. This naturally leads to the question: What relationship did Messiah have to the resurrection in Jewish thought? Can we find ideas of a suffering and rising Messiah? Could not Jesus as *Messiah* be expected to be raised from the dead? To such questions we turn in the next chapter.

NOTES

1. See R. H. Charles, *The Apocrypha and Pseudepigrapha of the Old Testament in English* (Oxford: Clarendon, 1913), 2 vols.
2. Josephus, *Jewish War* ii.8.14.
3. *Loc. cit.*
4. Sanhedrin X.1. See Mark 12: 18; Acts 23: 8.
5. See 2 Maccabees 7: 9, 11, 14, 22–23, 29; 12: 43.
6. There is a 2 Enoch, the date of whose composition is difficult to decide. It may be much later than the early Christian period.
7. See Helmer Ringgren, *The Faith of Qumran* (Philadelphia: Fortress, 1963), pp. 148–150.
8. See John Pryke, "Eschatology in the Dead Sea Scrolls," in *The Scrolls and Christianity*, ed. by M. Black (London: S.P.C.K., 1969), p. 56.
9. George Foot Moore, *Judaism in the First Centuries of the Christian Era* (Cambridge: Harvard, 1944), II, 379.
10. See George Eldon Ladd, "The Relevance of Apocalyptic for New Testament Theology," in *Reconciliation and Hope*, ed. by Robert Banks (Grand Rapids: Eerdmans, 1974).

CHAPTER 6

The Messiah and the Resurrection

WE HAVE SURVEYED the hope of the resurrection both in
the Old Testament and in Judaism. We have found the gradual
appearance of the idea of resurrection in the Old Testament.
We have also found that in Judaism there was great diversity
of thought. Certain circles believed in resurrection; others did
not. Some believed in the resurrection of a gross physical body;
others, in a transformed body. However, wherever resurrection
appears, *it is always eschatological.* It is resurrection at the end
of the age. We have found nothing in either the Old Testament
or contemporary Judaism to help us explain the rise of the
belief in the resurrection of Jesus.

However, the New Testament represents Jesus as the
Messiah. The New Testament pictures the early church as
believing that Jesus was the Messiah, and it also pictures Jesus
as believing himself to be the Messiah, but Messiah of the Son
of Man sort. This raises a further question. Was there anything
in either the Old Testament or in Judaism which expected
Messiah to suffer, die, and rise again? To answer this question,
we must survey the Hebrew and Jewish hope of the Messiah.

This raises an even more vital question. One of the critical
problems, as we have already seen, in the study of Jesus'
resurrection is the apparent contradiction that, according to
our Gospels, Jesus had on numerous occasions predicted his
death and resurrection; but after he was crucified, the disciples
are described as being utterly unprepared for that event. The
two disciples on the Emmaus road said, "We had hoped that
he was the one to redeem Israel" (Lk. 24: 21); but hope was

gone. Jesus was dead, and a dead man can do nothing, much less reign in the Kingdom of God.

Is this not a flat contradiction? Does this not mean that Jesus' predictions of his death are surely *vaticinia ex eventu* — prophecies after the event — formations of the early Christian church, and not historically trustworthy? Is it possible that Jesus on several occasions actually foretold his death and resurrection with complete lack of success in preparing his disciples for that event? Are we not to conclude that *neither* the disciples *nor* Jesus foresaw his death — much less his resurrection, and that the alleged predictions were put into the mouth of Jesus by the post-Easter community? We have already touched on this problem, but it demands thorough investigation.

On the other hand, could we not reverse the situation and argue that the rise of the resurrection faith can be easily explained from Jesus' predictions which in turn are based upon Old Testament prophecies of the suffering and death of Messiah? If one reads only the New Testament, one could easily conclude that the Old Testament was replete with such prophecies. Paul says that Christ not only died in accordance with the scriptures, but that "he was raised on the third day in accordance with the scriptures" (1 Cor. 15: 4). John comments on Peter's and John's state of mind on Easter morning: "for as yet they did not know the scripture, that he must rise from the dead" (Jn. 20: 19). Luke records that, on the Emmaus walk, Jesus rebuked the two disciples for being "slow of heart to believe all that the prophets have spoken . . . And beginning with Moses and all the prophets he interpreted to them in all the scriptures the things concerning himself" (Lk. 24: 25-27).

Again, did Jesus in his mission not fulfil the Old Testament prophecies in such a clear way that his disciples knew him to be Messiah, and as the divine Messiah, he must be the conqueror of death? This line of argument has assumed many forms. Long ago, the author of the most famous "life of Christ" wrote, "His death came to them not unexpectedly, but rather as of internal necessity and so the fulfilment of His often repeated prediction."[1]

The Gospels represent the disciples as hopeless after Jesus' death. When he appeared to them, they did not believe it was he. "They were startled and frightened, and supposed that they had seen a spirit" (Lk. 24: 37). John relates that on Easter evening, the disciples were gathered together behind shut doors "for fear of the Jews" (Jn. 20: 19). Thomas is reported as saying that he cannot believe the reports of the resurrection unless he can feel the hands and body of the resurrected Jesus for himself (Jn. 20: 25). Is such a negative attitude consistent with the Old Testament predictions of the Messiah and Jesus' own predictions of his suffering and death?

Modern Christians have no problem with this, for we read Isaiah 53 with its vivid depiction of a suffering, dying servant as a prophecy of the Messiah, and see Jesus' sufferings and death clearly foretold in the Old Testament.

To appreciate the proportions of this problem, we must try to think ourselves into the position of the disciples and to understand what their expectations were. To do this, we need to survey the Old Testament messianic prophecies and interpret them not through Christian eyes but in their own context and setting, as a first century Jew might do. In carrying out this task, we need to examine carefully the entire messianic concept as it appears in the Old Testament; and then we need to examine the contemporary messianic expectations of the Jews as they are reflected in the intertestamental literature. These writings are not canonical and carry no authority for Christian faith and practice, but they provide us with one of the most important sources to reconstruct first century Jewish thinking and expectation about the Messiah. It is true that we do not know exactly what circles in Judaism produced much of this literature, nor how widely the ideas reflected were held by first-century Jews; but they are the only sources we have, apart from the New Testament itself, to attempt to reconstruct first-century Jewish thought.[2]

There are three personages in the Old Testament who are interpreted in messianic terms in the New Testament: the Davidic King; the heavenly Son of Man, and the Suffering Servant. These three concepts are distinct and separate from each other, and are not conflated in the Old Testament. By this we mean to say that the Messiah is not the Son of Man, and the Suffering Servant is neither Messiah nor Son of Man.

The concept which appears most frequently is that of the Davidic King. We cannot here assemble and discuss all of the Old Testament references,[3] but we must discuss the most important representative passages.

The most familiar passages are in Isaiah 9 and 11. A child is to be born to rule in God's Kingdom. A close reading of Isaiah 9 shows that the king does not establish the Kingdom; he reigns in it after God has established it. He will rule from the throne of David for ever more (Isa. 9: 7). He will crush and destroy all that opposes his reign (vv. 4-5). His primary function is to establish universal peace and to rule in God's Kingdom. He will share the wisdom of God; in some unexplained way, he will even be a divine being. He will protect his people like a father; he will be the Prince of Peace (v. 6). While the king in some way is viewed as divine, this is no clear prophecy of the incarnation of the Son of God.

A similar picture is found in Isaiah 11. A new growth will spring forth from the fallen family of Jesse, the father of David. The Spirit of the Lord will give him great wisdom and understanding so that he can render true and not superficial judgments (vv. 2-3). Again, he does not establish the Kingdom, but reigns as the Davidic king in God's stead. "He shall smite the earth with the rod of his mouth, and with the breath of his lips he shall slay the wicked" (v. 4). The result of his reign will be peace in the entire creation. Violence and evil will be banished, "for the earth shall be full of the knowledge of the Lord as the waters cover the sea" (v. 9).

Here is the vivid expectation of a *mighty, conquering, invincible* Davidic king. This hope was dear to first-century Jewry, for we possess a collection of Psalms written in the late first century B.C. expressing precisely this hope. In 63 B.C., the Roman imperium in the person of Pompey invaded Palestine, captured Jerusalem, defiled the altar, and carried away captives. A short time thereafter, an unknown author penned these Psalms, including a prayer that God would send Israel "their king, the son of David". He will be known as "the anointed of the Lord" (literally, "the Lord's Christ"), and his mission will be to "destroy the pride of the sinner as a potter's vessel, with a rod of iron he shall break in pieces all their substance. He shall slay the godless nations with the word of his mouth."[4] He will purge Jerusalem of her pollutions by the Gentiles, exalting the holy city over all other nations; he will gather together a holy people—Israel—under his rule, and will make all heathen nations to serve him under his yoke. Through this Davidic king—the Lord's Messiah—the Lord himself will become Israel's king for ever and ever.

In brief, "Messiah" was a Davidic king who would arise from among men but would be supernaturally endowed to destroy the national and political enemies of Israel and to gather God's people—Israel—into the earthly Kingdom of God with Jerusalem as its capital. In light of this, we can understand why Jesus never publicly proclaimed himself to be Messiah. After the miracle of the feeding of the five thousand, the people wanted to take Jesus by force and make him (messianic) king; but Jesus withdrew from the crowd. The meaning is clear. Here was a man endowed with supernatural powers; against such a mighty leader, the Roman legions must fall. Here was the one who could establish by divine power the divine rule and bring Israel into the Kingdom.

Jesus was the Messiah, but he was not that kind of Messiah. Peter's confession (Mk. 8: 29) was an amazing assertion. It indicated that the disciples were beginning to understand Jesus' novel messiahship, but that their understanding was very rudimentary and defective. One thing is clear. Jesus was not the kind of messianic king the Jews were looking for. Messiah, by definition, was one who would destroy his enemies, save Israel, and establish God's all-encompassing rule on the earth. He would be the political and social saviour of Israel. How could this Messiah possibly suffer and die? In light of this background, Peter's confession of Jesus' messiahship was an amazing event. This knowledge could be gained only by revelation, not by human observation (Mt. 16: 17). There is no background in this messianic hope for a dying and rising Messiah.

A second messianic concept is that of Son of Man. Daniel saw a vision of the heavenly throne room with the "Ancient of Days" seated on his throne. Then there flew "one like a son of man" with the clouds of heaven to the Ancient of Days to receive the Kingdom of God. Then, apparently, he descends from heaven with the right to rule, establishes God's Kingdom on the earth, and reigns for ever with the saints of the Most

High (Dan. 7: 13-14, 26-27). The question as to whether or not the Son of Man is a corporate or individual figure need not concern us here; he seems to be an individual figure who represents the saints of God. Son of Man is not here a messianic title, although we have used it as such, because in later writing, including the Gospels, it becomes a messianic title.

The book of Enoch (first to second century B.C.) picks up this Son of Man idea and enlarges on it. In Enoch, the Son of Man is clearly an individual, pre-existent, supra-human being who comes to earth to destroy the wicked, preside over the resurrection of the dead, hold the final judgment, and reign for ever in God's Kingdom.[5]

The Son of Man is therefore essentially a heavenly, eschatological personage who will come from heaven at the end of the age to superintend the events accompanying the establishment of God's eternal Kingdom.[6]

In light of this background Jesus' use of Son of Man was utterly novel and perplexing. It was his favourite term to designate himself. He used the term in three different ways. He was the Son of Man on earth, serving the will of God (see Mk. 2: 10; 2: 28; Mt. 8: 20). Whoever heard of the heavenly Son of Man appearing on earth as a mere man among men? This was indeed confusing. A recent technical book argues that Jesus' use of Son of Man embodies a clear claim to heavenly pre-existence.[7] This we believe; but if so, this meaning was lost on the people, for the Son of Man in Judaism was never thought to descend from heaven to live as a man among men. When he comes, it will be with heavenly power and glory to disrupt the present evil age and establish the eternal Kingdom of God.

After Peter's confession at Caesarea Philippi, Jesus began to teach two new things about the Son of Man. First, he must suffer and die (Mk. 8: 31; 9: 12, 30; 10: 33) and then come with the glory of his Father in the eschatological Kingdom of God (Mk. 8: 38; 13: 26). If Jesus had taught *only* that some day the Son of Man would come in glory to establish God's Kingdom, his message would have been understood, for he would have said no more than Daniel and Enoch say. But that *he* was the Son of Man on earth as a man among men, and especially that as the Son of Man he must suffer and die —

this was unheard of, *and seemed to be a contradiction in terms*. How could a celestial glorious being become the helpless victim of lawless men and die the death of a criminal?

Here is the historical explanation for the disciples' utter inability to grasp Jesus' predictions about suffering, death, and resurrection. It was a flat contradiction of everything they believed about Messiah and Son of Man. He was to conquer and reign, not suffer and die. The two ideas were mutually exclusive. He was to destroy the wicked, not be destroyed by the wicked. He was to establish the Kingdom of God, not fall victim to the kingdoms of men.

In all fairness, we must note that some scholars find the idea of a suffering Son of Man in Daniel 7. They point out that the Son of Man represents the saints, and before the Son of Man comes in glory, the saints are persecuted by the four beasts. "The Son of Man, before coming into glory, suffers, and his sufferings are, historically, the sufferings of the martyrs."[8] This is, however, a minority opinion; and it is clear from the apocalypse of Enoch that the Jews did not understand the Son of Man to be a suffering servant.

There remains a third "messianic" concept—that of the Suffering Servant in Isaiah 53. This passage was interpreted as referring to the Messiah by the New Testament church (Mt. 12:18-21; Acts 7:32ff), but in *its own Old Testament context*, it was not a prophecy of the Messiah. It pictures an unnamed Suffering Servant who will redeem his people by his sufferings and death (Isa. 53:9, 12). As a matter of fact, Isaiah 53 speaks not about Messiah, who is a conquering Davidic King, but about a servant of the Lord (Isa. 52:13). This chapter is one of several servant passages; and in earlier references the servant is explicitly designated as the people Israel (see Isa. 49:3; 48:20; 45:4; 44:21; 44:1; 43:1). Furthermore it is of greatest importance to know that Judaism before Christ never interpreted this passage as referring to the sufferings of Messiah. An expert in Jewish literature says, "In the whole Jewish Messianic literature of the Tannaitic period [before A.D. 200] there is no trace of the 'suffering Messiah'."[9] Isaiah 53 was thought to tell of the sufferings of God's people, Israel; and this interpretation can be found in modern Jewish interpreters. "The *whole* people of *Israel in the form of the elect of the nation* gradually became *the Messiah of the world, the redeemer of mankind.*"[10] Later Judaism came to interpret Isaiah 53 messianically as the Targum of Isaiah shows.[11] This Aramaic translation stems from the fifth century A.D. While the servant is the Messiah, the text of Isaiah 53 is so radically distorted that the Servant-Messiah is to scatter and crush the wicked Gentiles, to emancipate Israel, to rebuild the temple, to subject many rebels to the law. The disfigurement, the oppression, the humiliation, the suffering for guilt of which the passage speaks was transferred from the Servant-Messiah either to Israel, or to the wicked nations.[12]

Here we have a phenomenon which is common in the New Testament use of the Old Testament. A text is reinterpreted and a deeper messianic meaning found in it in light of the Christ event than appears in the Old Testament context. In its own historical context, the Suffering Servant is both the nation and an unnamed individual who stands in solidarity with the nation as a whole and redeems the nation by his vicarious sufferings. In the New Testament, this is seen to be a prophecy of the sufferings of the Messiah. However, in Judaism, the Messiah continues to be a victorious deliverer of Israel, not a Suffering Servant.

One further point must be noted. In the servant passage in Isaiah 53, the servant is delivered from death and vindicated. "He shall see his offspring, he shall prolong his days; the will of the Lord shall prosper in his hand; he shall see the fruit of the travail of his soul and be satisfied" (Isa. 53: 10-11). Here in some sense of the word is victory over death, and it could be interpreted in terms of the resurrection of the Servant who has poured out his soul into death. The important thing to note is that the New Testament *never appeals to this passage to support the resurrection of Jesus*. This is rather surprising, for we may assume that after Jesus' death and resurrection, his disciples combed the scriptures to find biblical support for these new redemptive events. But the fact is that neither the early church nor Judaism appealed to this passage to support the idea of resurrection of Messiah.

In two first century A.D. apocalypses, the heavenly Son of Man and the Davidic Messiah are clearly conflated. The Apocalypse of Ezra, or 4 Ezra, is an apocalypse written after the fall of Jerusalem by a deeply sensitive Jew who cannot understand why Israel, faithful to the Law, has fallen upon such evil times. While the author wrestles with this problem from various points of view, his final answer is in eschatology. This age is under the relentless control of evil powers, and God's people, righteous though they are, can expect nothing but suffering. However, at the end of this evil age, God will intervene to punish the wicked and reward the righteous in a blessed Age to Come. The agent of this redemption will be "my son the Messiah [who] shall be revealed with those who are with him, and those who remain shall rejoice four hundred years. And after these years my son the Messiah shall die, and all who draw human breath. And the world shall be turned to primeval silence for seven days, as it was at the first beginnings; so that no one shall be left" (4 Ez. 7: 28-30).[13] After the seven days of silence, the Age to Come will be inaugurated; corruption shall perish; the dead will be raised, both the righteous and the wicked; God will hold judgment; the wicked will be sent to the furnace of hell, while the righteous will enter into the paradise of delight in the Age to Come (4 Ez. 7: 31-44).

Several facts are notable. The messianic figure is called both "my son" and "Messiah". We cannot be sure what the original words rendered "my son" were, for the original semitic text was first rendered into Greek, which in turn was translated into several near eastern languages, including Latin. Only the second-hand translations are extant, and we do not know what word was used either in the Hebrew-Aramaic or in Greek for "my son". However, in the Old Testament, "my son" can be used of the eschatological messianic king (Ps. 2: 2, 7). The important thing is that he is called "Messiah", but instead of being born among men of the family of David, he is "revealed"; i.e., he comes from heaven like the Son of Man. He is accompanied by men like Enoch and Elijah who had been caught up to heaven without dying (4 Ez. 6: 26). The text does not say that the Messiah brings the Kingdom; nor is the fact emphasised that he reigns in the Kingdom, although this may be assumed. Here is the clearest passage in Jewish literature which speaks of a temporal earthly kingdom before the establishment of the Kingdom in the eternal Age to Come.

At the end of this "messianic" kingdom, all human beings die, including God's son, the Messiah. *Here is the one passage in Jewish intertestamental literature which speaks of a dying Messiah.* However, he dies, he does not suffer. He lives an unusually long life of four hundred years and then dies with the rest of men. His death has no theological significance. While he is a heavenly being like the Son of Man, he is a mortal being like the Messiah. After his death, he disappears from sight. Apparently, he is raised from the dead along with the righteous to enjoy the blessing of the Age to Come, but his presence is not noted. The most important fact is that while he dies, he dies simply as a man, not as the Suffering Servant of Isaiah 53.

In the same apocalypse, we find another passage where the Son of Man comes to destroy the enemies of God's people. He is again called God's son. "My son" is revealed as a man coming up out of the sea. The pagan nations gather together to conquer him; but he will stand on the top of Mount Zion, and the Messiah will destroy them without effort by the law. The meaning of his coming from the sea is given: "Just as no one can explore or know what is in the depths of the sea, so no one on earth can see my son *or those who are with him until the time of his day*" (4 Ez. 13: 52). He is the one "whom the Most High has been keeping for many ages, who will himself deliver his creation; and he will direct those who are left" (4 Ez. 13: 26). This is another way of describing the heavenly pre-existent Messiah of the Apocalypse of Enoch. Here the Son of Man neither suffers or dies. He destroys the enemies of God's people and gathers together the ten tribes (4 Ez. 13: 40) of Israel which had been scattered among the nations into the Kingdom of God.

In another chapter, the eschatological redeemer is clearly a synthesis of the Davidic Messiah and the heavenly Son of Man. Ezra sees a vision of an eagle which clearly represents the Roman Empire which reigned "over the earth and over those who dwell in it" (11: 5), afflicting the meek and injuring the peaceable (11: 42). Then he sees a lion aroused out of the forest who spoke with a man's voice to announce the eagle's doom. The lion is the Messiah "whom the Most High has kept until the end of days, who will arise from the posterity of David" (12: 32). He will first reprove the wicked in judgment, "and when he has reproved them, then he will destroy them"

(12: 33). Then he will "deliver in mercy the servant of my people" (12: 34). Then he will gather those who have survived the messianic woes into a temporal earthly kingdom "until the end comes, the day of judgment" (12: 34). In this expectation, 4 Ezra 12 is similar to 4 Ezra 7. However, there is no resurrection in this passage.

Here, the Messiah both arises from the seed of David—i.e., he is a human being—and he is kept in heaven until the end of days—i.e., he is the heavenly pre-existent Son of Man. One commentor explains this fact in these words: "here the, originally Jewish, belief in a transcendental and an earthly Messiah coalesce through the Christian doctrine of the dual nature of Christ."[14] However, it is unlikely that Christian thought influenced Judaism at this early date, particularly in the doctrine of the dual nature of Christ which had not been explicitly formulated in the first century. It is more likely that this represents an independent fusion of what had been different stands of messianic tradition.

In another apocalypse, Baruch,[15] the "Messiah" is revealed to men and the kingdom is established on earth. After the kingdom, the Messiah "will return in glory", apparently to heaven. There follows the resurrection of the righteous and the eternal Kingdom in the Age to Come (Apoc. Bar. 29: 3–30:3), while the souls of the wicked waste away in torment.

In the vision just described, the Messiah does not play an active role; but in another vision the Messiah first destroys "the last leader", probably the Antichrist, and rules on earth in a temporal kingdom (Apoc. Bar. 40: 1-4). Again, the rule of the Messiah is "revealed" (39: 7).

In yet another vision, the Messiah is a warrior who slays his enemies; but he will spare the nations that have not known Israel or have not trodden down the seed of Jacob; but all who have ruled over God's people shall be slain with the sword (Apoc. Bar. 72).

We have completed our survey and are in a position to understand not only why the disciples were unable to understand Jesus' predictions about his death and resurrection but also why they had difficulty with Jesus' mission as Messiah.

Let us treat the last question first. Both Messiah and Son of

Man in the Old Testament and in Judaism were eschatological figures associated with the establishment of the Kingdom of God, the gathering of Israel into the Kingdom, and the judgment and punishment of the wicked. John the Baptist announced the coming of such an apocalyptic figure. The coming one would baptise both in the Holy Spirit—salvation, and in the fire of judgment. He would gather the wheat into the granary and burn up the chaff with unquenchable fire (Mt. 3:11-12). Little wonder that when Jesus failed to do anything of the sort—when John himself was rotting in prison under the tyranny of Herod Antipas—that John sent to Jesus with the question, "Are you he who is to come, or shall we look for another?" (Mt. 11:3). The "deeds of the Messiah" (Mt. 11:2) were not what John expected—salvation for the righteous and judgment for wicked men like Herod. Instead, Jesus was performing such good works as giving sight to the blind, hearing to the deaf, cleansing to lepers, and even life to the dead. The point is: in spite of Isaiah 35:5-6, *these were not thought of as the "deeds of Messiah"*. This is why the disciples were perplexed about Jesus' messiahship. Unquestionably he had miraculous powers, but he was not establishing the glorious Kingdom of God among men.

Furthermore, when Jesus began to teach that as the Son of Man his mission was to suffer and die (Mt. 8:31), the disciples were sure something was wrong. The Son of Man by definition was a heavenly super-human being who would come to earth with power and glory to transform the present order and reign in God's glorious Kingdom. But a suffering and dying Son of Man—such a thing was unheard of. It was in fact a contradiction in terms. Son of Man was to conquer and reign, not to die.

This is the point: *it was completely hidden from the disciples that the Son of Man must fill the role of the Suffering Servant of Isaiah 53 before he comes in the power and glory of God's Kingdom.* We must not forget: in all Jewish literature, there is a dying Messiah only in 4 Ezra 7, and there, his death has no saving power. A suffering and dying Messiah or Son of Man was unheard of and seemed to be a flat contradiction to the explicit Word of God.

In light of these facts, the Gospel story is psychologically sound. The disciples were slow to recognise in Jesus their

Messiah, for by his actions he was fulfilling none of the roles expected for the Messiah. In fact, when the people tried to force his hand, Jesus drew back. After feeding five thousand people with a few loaves and fishes, the people wanted to take Jesus by force and make him their king (Jn. 6: 15) — i.e., Messiah. Give him a few swords and shields, and he could equip an army. Even the Roman legions could not stand before such divine power. When, instead of offering swords and shields, Jesus offered his body and blood (Jn. 6: 53), "many of his disciples drew back and no longer went about with him" (Jn. 6: 66). When challenged, Peter replied, "to whom shall we go? You have the words of eternal life" (Jn. 6: 68); but in saying this, Peter said far more than he understood.

Thus we may conclude that our Gospels are both historically and psychologically sound. Jesus' predictions did not adequately condition his disciples for his death. The Old Testament prophets do not predict the sufferings and death of either Messiah or Son of Man, but of an unnamed, undesignated Suffering Servant. Contemporary Jewish literature does not reflect the hope of a suffering redeemer. In fact, Jesus' mission of suffering and death was contradictory to everything the disciples knew about Messiah. Something had to *happen* to create their resurrection faith that the crucified, dead Messiah had returned to life.

NOTES

1. Alfred Edersheim, *The Life and Times of Jesus the Messiah* (New York: Longmans, Green, 1886), II, 624.
2. The literature found at Qumran does not contain ideas that are of any help to us in this quest.
3. This is done by E. Jenni in the article "Messiah, Jewish" in the *Interpreter's Dictionary of the Bible*, K–Q, pp. 360–365.
4. These quotations will be found in Psalms of Solomon 17 in R. H. Charles, *The Apocrypha and Pseudepigrapha of the Old Testament in English* (Oxford, Clarendon, 1913), II, pp. 649–650.
5. This picture will be found in the ch. 37–71 in R. H. Charles, *op. cit.*, II, pp. 208–236. We should note in passing that fragments of parts 1, 3, 4 and 5 of Enoch have been found in Qumran, but fragments from the Similitudes are missing. This has led some scholars to the conclusion that the Similitudes are a Christian work. However, we agree with Jeremias who points out that the Similitudes are completely lacking in

Christian features (J. Jeremias, *New Testament Theology* [London: S.C.M. Press, 1971], I, p. 269) and therefore must be considered Jewish.

6. In two passages in Enoch, The Son of Man is called "Messiah" (48: 10 and 52: 4). This suggests that the two concepts are beginning to conflate. But in general, it is best to see two distinctly different personages.

7. R. G. Hammerton-Kelly. *Pre-existence, Wisdom and the Son of Man* (Cambridge University Press, 1973).

8. See C. K. Barrett, "The Background of Mark 10: 45," in *New Testament Essays*, ed. by A. J. B. Higgins (Manchester University Press, 1959), p. 14.

9. Joseph Klausner, *The Messianic Idea in Israel* (New York: Macmillan, 1955), p. 405.

10. *Ibid.*, p. 163.

11. A targum is an Aramaic paraphrastic translation of the Hebrew Old Testament text.

12. A translation of this targum will be found in Wm. Manson, *Jesus the Messiah* (Philadelphia: Westminster, 1946), pp. 229–232, and in G. Kittel's *Theological Dictionary of the New Testament* (Grand Rapids: Eerdmans, 1967), V, pp. 693–694. Jeremias, who wrote the article in Kittel, thinks he can trace the idea of a suffering messiah back to pre-Christian times, but this is by no means clear. However, Jeremias admits that the violent treatment of the text of Isaiah by the targum is due to anti-Christian polemic. *Ibid.*, p. 695.

13. The text will be found in modern editions of the Apocrypha such as that edited by Bruce M. Metzger (New York: Oxford, 1965) and with introduction and notes in R. H. Charles, *op. cit.*, II, pp. 542–624. Quotations here are from Metzger's edition which serves as a supplement to the R.S.V.

14. W. O. E. Oesterley, *II Esdras* (London: Methuen, 1933), p. 141.

15. The text will be found in R. H. Charles, *op. cit.*, II, pp. 470–526. It is approximately contemporary with 4 Ezra.

CHAPTER 7

The Nature of the Gospels

IT IS TIME to consider the witness of the four Gospels to the resurrection of Jesus. We have already seen that there is textual reason to believe in the basic integrity of the Gospels' report of the teachings of Jesus.[1]

We must first say something about the nature of the Gospels. The older "uncritical" view held that they were eyewitness accounts of the life and deeds of Jesus and are therefore completely trustworthy as authentic historical records. This view is no longer possible, for present-day scholars almost universally recognise that the Gospels were not produced until at least thirty to forty years after the events they record, and that the tradition about the life and words of Jesus was preserved in oral form for at least a generation before it was written down.[2] Furthermore, it is almost universally recognised that the early church *shaped* the oral tradition to meet its particular needs; and the most recent scholarship has emphasised that the authors of the Gospels were no mere purveyors of tradition but were theologians in their own right.[3] This means that the Gospels are not pure, "objective" history, if "objective" means the work of detached, disinterested authors. Each evangelist *selected* his material and to some degree *shaped* his material to suit his particular theological and ecclesiastical interests. This means that we are not to expect strict wooden agreement among the Gospels. It is obvious that the Evangelists are often relatively little concerned about such strict historical matters as time, place, sequence of events, and the like, which would be quite important in strictly historical documents. They are concerned to give us portraits of who Jesus was and what he said and did. The important critical question is: Did they succeed in accomplishing their purpose?

At this point, contemporary criticism diverges into different streams of thought. The most radical contemporary critic is Bultmann. He admits that the Gospels portray Jesus as a divine man. However, since every "modern man", Bultmann would say, knows that the category of divine men belongs to mythology and not to history, the Gospels are quite unreliable historically. The Gospels are witnesses to what the church believed about Jesus, not pictures of Jesus as he actually was. The real "historical Jesus"—that is, the merely human Jesus—is lost behind the tradition of the divine Christ. In other words, not only the selection and form of the Gospels was created by the early church; the very substance of the Gospels is a community product, not accurate history.

Such critics view the Gospels as the end product of a free-floating oral tradition whose substance was rather completely transformed in the course of its preservation. For such scholars, the stories of the resurrection are largely legendary and mythological. Thus Bultmann says that the stories of the empty tomb are an apologetic legend designed to prove the resurrection of Jesus.[4]

Most critics recognise a higher level of credibility in the Gospels. While the Gospels themselves are the formulation of oral tradition, this tradition was always under the control of eyewitnesses which renders the main features of their witness credible. The authorship of the first Gospel—Matthew—is an unsolved enigma. However, our earliest Gospel is Mark. An early witness to Mark—that of Papias (c. A.D. 130)—affirms that Mark was the attendant of Peter in Rome and that his Gospel was based on the reminiscences of Peter. While many critics completely discount this external witness, it cannot be easily dismissed. Martin, who is primarily concerned with redaction criticism, carefully weighs Papias' evidence and concludes that it is basically sound. Mark was probably written around A.D. 65 in Rome by Mark, the attendant of Peter. Martin concludes that

. . . in Mark the evangelist we have a writer who "had

considerable opportunities of gathering knowledge of the kind that would later be useful in the composition of the Gospel," through his association with the leading apostles both in Jerusalem, in Antioch and in Rome. . . . Mark became Peter's "interpreter" by publishing his gospel in which he recorded Peter's teaching.[5]

While many scholars date Luke-Acts very late in the first or early in the second century by an unknown Christian, it is far more probable that Luke-Acts was written by Luke, the companion of Paul, and was written a little earlier than the Neronic persecution of the Christians in A.D. 64.[6] If Luke was with Paul during his Caesarean imprisonment, as the "we" sections suggest (Acts 21 : 18; 27 : 1), he had ample opportunity in Palestine to familiarise himself with the main events of Jesus' life, death, and resurrection from men who had been "from the beginning . . . eyewitnesses and ministers of the word" (Lk. 1 : 2).

The date and authorship of the Fourth Gospel is a more difficult problem. Tradition attributes the Fourth Gospel to the apostle John, and this position still is defensible.[7] Until twenty-five or so years ago, "advanced" critics saw almost nothing of historical value in this Gospel. However, there is a contemporary shift in Johannine criticism so that the Gospel has taken on a "new look".[8] One of our most painstaking English scholars has undertaken a fresh study of the Johannine tradition and concludes, "Behind the Fourth Gospel lies an ancient tradition independent of the other gospels and meriting serious consideration as a contribution of our knowledge of the historical facts concerning Jesus Christ."[9] With specific reference to the Johannine resurrection stories, Dodd finds an independent oral tradition which was formulated substantially before A.D. 66 in Palestine,[10] that is, well within the period when eyewitnesses were still in the church.

We conclude that while the Gospels were not written by eyewitnesses of Jesus, they embody a tradition which in its oral form was under the control of eyewitnesses. We concur with the judgment of Vincent Taylor, "If the Form-Critics are right, the disciples must have been translated to heaven immediately after the Resurrection."[11] However, disciples of Jesus continued in the church and must have exercised control over the tradition at its most important points. The role of eyewitnesses to Jesus is defended by many competent scholars today.[12] If this be true, we may expect to find variation in unimportant details, but a sound memory as to the major events. Here, I am speaking as a historian in terms of historical probability.

I may be permitted to give a personal illustration. In April of 1958, I was in Lisbon, Portugal, where one evening I attended the dedication of a new Baptist church. I can still vividly remember the grey apartment house which held a large room where some hundred people were gathered. I can remember the orangeish light which illuminated the room. I do not remember the preacher or the sermon. After returning to America, I referred to this event and mentioned its occurring on a Sunday evening. My wife said to me, "George, why don't you get your dates straight? It was on a Friday night, not Sunday." Friday or Sunday—that was unimportant to the purpose for which I told the story. I was wrong in the date, but I was in no way wrong about the fact that I was in Lisbon and myself witnessed the birth of a new Baptist church.

With this as background, let us turn to the Gospels to examine closely their witness to the resurrection.

NOTES

1. See above, p. 36.
2. See G. E. Ladd, *The New Testament and Criticism* (Grand Rapids: Eerdmans, 1967), ch. VI, "Form Criticism."
3. The latter method is called "redaction criticism" from the German *Redaktionskritik*.
4. R. Bultmann, *The History of the Synoptic Tradition* (Oxford: Basil Blackwell, 1963), p. 287.
5. Ralph P. Martin, *Mark: Evangelist and Theologian* (Grand Rapids: Zondervan, 1973), p. 61. See Martin's discussion of the entire problem, pp. 52–63. Martin's quotation is from T. W. Manson.
6. See F. F. Bruce, *The Book of the Acts* (Grand Rapids: Eerdmans, 1954), p. 22.
7. See Leon Morris, *Commentary on the Gospel of John* (Grand Rapids: Eerdmans, 1971), pp. 8–29.
8. See A. M. Hunter, *According to John. The New Look at the Fourth Gospel* (Philadelphia: Westminster, 1968).

9. C. H. Dodd, *Historical Tradition in the Fourth Gospel* (Cambridge: University Press, 1963), p. 423.
10. *Op. cit.*, p. 150.
11. Vincent Taylor, *The Formation of the Gospel Tradition* (London: Macmillan, 1935), p. 41.
12. See F. V. Filson, *A New Testament History* (Philadelphia: Westminster, 1964), p. 78; F. F. Bruce in *Jesus of Nazareth: Saviour and Lord* (Grand Rapids: Eerdmans, 1966), pp. 98, 100; Oscar Cullmann, *Salvation in History* (New York: Harper & Row, 1967), pp. 90, 98 *et passim*; Bruce M. Metzger, *The New Testament* (New York/Nashville: Abingdon, 1965), p. 87; James L. Price, *Interpreting the New Testament* (New York; Holt, Rinehart and Winston, 1961), p. 159.

CHAPTER 8

The Witness of the Gospels

THE MOST CASUAL READING of the resurrection account of the four gospels will show that they embody great diversity. In fact, one of the major problems in the contemporary study of the gospels is this diversity, which is so great as to seem to amount to flat contradiction among the four accounts. This has often led to the easy conclusion that since the Gospels appear to be contradictory in reporting these alleged events, they are quite unreliable as history. For instance, a recent study of the resurrection says,

> The best way to discredit a witness in court is for the cross-examiner to tie him up in knots and make his evidence appear to be such a tissue of inconsistencies that the jury becomes convinced he is untrustworthy. *One does not need to be a scientific New Testament scholar to do that with the resurrection narratives* (italics ours).[1]

We have no desire to gloss over the difficulty of the problem, and the following chart on pages 80–82 sets forth an analysis of the resurrection events, showing the areas of agreement and disagreement.

Before we discuss this problem, a preliminary difficulty must be faced to which no certain answer can be given. The oldest text of Mark does not relate any appearances of the resurrected Jesus. The "long ending", consisting of 16: 9-19, which appears in our Authorised Version, is in fact only one of *five* endings of

Agreements in ordinary print; disagreements in italics.

	MATTHEW	MARK	LUKE	JOHN
1.	*toward the dawn of the first day*	*when Sabbath was past*	on the first day of the week	on the first day of the week
2.	women	women	women	women
3.	Mary Magdalene, *the other Mary*	Mary Magdalene *Mary, mother of Salome*	Mary Magdalene *Mary, mother of James; Joanna*	Mary Magdalene *(alone)*
4.	*to see the tomb*	*to anoint Jesus' body*	*taking spices*	*no reason given (Nicodemus anoints the body, 19:39)*
5.	*an earthquake* *an angel* rolled the stone	they found the stone rolled away	they found the stone rolled back	found the stone taken away
6.	*an angel*	*a young man*	*two men*	*two angels (20:12)*
7.	*the guards fall like dead men*			
8.		the women enter the empty tomb	they did not find the body	
9.	"He has risen, as he said"	"He has risen, he is not here"	"Why do you seek the living among the dead?"	

	MATTHEW	MARK	LUKE	JOHN
				Mary runs to tell Peter and the other disciple
10.	"Go, tell his disciples"	"Go, tell his disciples and Peter"		
11.	"He is going before you to Galilee; there you will see him."	"He is going before you to Galilee; there you will see him."		
12.	They departed quickly with fear and joy	They fled trembling and astonished	They returned from the tomb	
13.	They ran to tell his disciples	They said nothing to anyone; they were afraid	They told all this to the eleven and all the rest. They do not believe	
14.	*Jesus meets the two women*			
15.				*Peter and John enter the empty tomb; Peter believes (21:3-10)*
16.				*Jesus appears to Mary (21:11-17)*
17.				*Mary tells the disciples*
18.			*appearance to two disciples near Emmaus*	

	MATTHEW	MARK	LUKE	JOHN
19.			*an appearance to the eleven in Jerusalem (24: 36-49)*	*an appearance to the disciples (20: 19-23)*
20.				*a second appearance to the eleven, including Thomas (20: 21-29)*
21.				*an appearance in Tiberias (21: 1-23)*
22.	*the great commission in Galilee*			
23.			*the ascension from Bethany*	

Mark in the manuscript tradition. Modern scholarship is almost unanimously agreed that verses 9-19 were not part of the original gospel but were added at an early date because it was recognised that Mark ended abruptly with no appearances of the risen Jesus. However, at this point, unanimity of opinion ends. Many scholars feel that the ending of the gospel of Mark was mutilated at an early date when it was extant in only one manuscript, and that the gospel originally contained a lost page, now irretrievably lost, which recorded appearances of the resurrected Jesus. Many other scholars argue that Mark wrote as an artist and deliberately concluded his gospel on a note of expectant fear. A vigorous debate has taken place as to whether a proper Greek sentence could end with the structure of 16: 8: *ephobounto gar*—the latter word being a conjunction; and the debate has received no positive answer. The question is to be answered purely as a matter of critical judgment.

The present author has never been impressed by the arguments about Mark's literary artistry. It seems altogether likely that Mark would have related appearances of the risen Jesus. His gospel frequently refers to the resurrection, which proves that the resurrection was an important event in his thinking. After Peter's confession of Jesus as the Messiah at Caesarea Philippi, Jesus told the disciples that he must be rejected and killed, "and after three days rise again" (Mk. 8: 31). After the transfiguration, Jesus charged the disciples "to tell no one what they had seen, until the Son of man should have risen from the dead" (Mk. 9: 9). This one verse indicates that the resurrection was indeed a watershed in the understanding of Jesus' person and mission. Again, Jesus foretold his death and resurrection a second time (Mk. 9: 31); "but they did not understand the saying, and they were afraid to ask him" (Mk. 9: 32). On yet a third occasion, according to Mark, Jesus announced that it was his mission as the Son of Man to "give his life as a ransom for many" (Mk. 10: 45)—a mission that would be obviously meaningless if he remained dead. Again, on Easter morning, Mark relates that when the women came to the tomb, a young man announced to them, "Do not be amazed; you seek Jesus of Nazareth, who was crucified. He has risen, he is not here. See the place where they laid him" (Mk. 16: 6).

All this proves that the resurrection was not unimportant to Mark; and this makes it highly improbable that Mark would have told the Easter story without relating appearances of the risen Jesus. We conclude that Mark 16: 8 is a mutilated ending of the gospel; but this is only a supposition which lacks proof. It really matters little for our purpose, for whatever the facts may be, *our* Mark ends at 16: 9, and we cannot guess what he would have written in a further record.

One fact is clear. Our gospels represent distinctly different traditions. One of the "facts" of modern New Testament critisism is that Mark is the oldest gospel and that Matthew and Luke made use of Mark.[2] However, in the resurrection accounts, both Matthew and Luke go their own ways, forsaking their source. In the two brief passages where Matthew and Mark are parallel (Mt. 28: 1, 5-8), there are only a few words reflecting interdependence. All this means that *at the points in which the gospels agree, that agreement is all the more striking*.

There are numerous divergences between the Gospels which are more or less typical of the gospels as a whole. The names of the women differ. The three synoptics mention Mary Magdalene and Mary, the mother of James. Mark in addition mentions Salome (see Mt. 27: 56). Luke mentions Joanna (see Lk. 8: 3). These are not serious divergences. It is more difficult when John mentions only Mary Magdalene as though she were alone. It is not impossible, however, that a group of women came early to the tomb and found the stone rolled away; whereupon Mary rushed off to tell Peter and John while the other women stayed in the garden.

A more serious difficulty is met in the statements about the purpose of the women's visit to the tomb. Mark (16: 1), followed by Luke (24: 1), tell us that they came with spices to anoint the body of Jesus. However, John tells us that Nicodemus had already anointed Jesus' body before laying it in the tomb (Jn. 19: 39-40). Whether this represents faulty tradition, or whether the women came to complete an anointing which Nicodemus had begun, we cannot say. Furthermore, many critics point to the unnatural situation in which the women would anoint a body which had been dead for two nights and a day, especially since the tomb was sealed with a heavy stone; but Cranfield aptly remarks that "love often prompts people to do what from a practical view is useless."[3]

Another apparent contradiction is the statement in John that Jesus was wrapped in strips of linen cloth (*othonioi*, Jn. 19: 40) whereas all three synoptics say that Jesus was wrapped in a linen shroud (*sindōn*) — a large sheet of cloth (Mk. 15: 46ff.). The traditional harmonisation is that the body was first wrapped in a shroud after being taken down from the cross; but before being left in the tomb, the shroud was torn into strips which were used to bind the body, limb by limb, between layers of myrrh and aloes.[4] Possibly the body was first wrapped in a shroud and then strips of cloth were wound around the shrouded body.

A more serious difficulty is found in the fact that the Synoptics relate the visit of several women while John seems to know only of the visit of Mary. However, this may not be an outright contradiction, for when Mary met Peter and "the other disciple" to relate her experience, she said, "They have taken the Lord out of the tomb, and *we* do not know where they have laid him" (Jn. 20: 2). So it is possible that because it was Mary alone who ran on ahead to tell Peter and the beloved disciple that she alone is mentioned in the Fourth Gospel.[5]

Another minor discrepancy is the response of the women to the announcement of the angel that Jesus had risen. Mark's abrupt ending tells us that they fled from the tomb "for trembling and astonishment had come upon them; and they said nothing to anyone, for they were afraid" (Mk. 16: 8). On the other hand, both Matthew and Luke say that they "departed quickly from the tomb with fear and great joy, and ran to tell his disciples" (Mt. 28: 8; see Lk. 24: 9). However, Matthew also relates that as the women were on their way from the tomb to the city, Jesus met them, and they took hold of his feet and worshipped him. Then Jesus repeated the command for his disciples to go into Galilee where Jesus would meet them (Mt. 28: 9-10). It is possible that the initial reaction of the women was fear (Matthew says it was both fear and joy) and only after meeting Jesus did they go to tell the disciples what they had seen. On the other hand, this may be one of the unimportant discrepancies which mark the Synoptic Gospels. If Matthew and Luke had Mark before them as they wrote, they knew that they were changing his narrative. Perhaps the problem would be easily solved if we possessed the "lost ending" of Mark.

The most foreboding problem is that of the locale of the appearances of the resurrected Jesus to his disciples. Mark does not relate any appearances because of the defective ending of his gospel, but when the "young man" told Mary Magdalene that "he is going before you into Galilee; there you will see him as he told you" (Mk. 16: 4), it seems best to understand the verse as a promise of a resurrection appearance or appearances in Galilee, and to suppose that Jesus wished to meet his disciples in Galilee.[6] Matthew, in one of the few places where his gospel follows the exact wording of Mark in the resurrection narrative, records the same command (Mt. 28: 7). Matthew also records that the eleven disciples went to Galilee where Jesus met them and gave them the "Great Commission" to make disciples of all nations (Mt. 28: 16-19). In addition, Matthew records an appearance to the women in Jerusalem which is not recorded in either Mark or Luke.

On the other hand, Luke records appearances only in or near Jerusalem. He omits the command of the angel recorded by both Mark and Matthew that Jesus will precede his disciples to Galilee. He records at considerable length the story of Jesus' appearance to two disciples on the road to Emmaus. Evans thinks that this is "the account of a resurrection appearance which may be called a 'legend' in the technical sense of a story of a supernatural being who companies naturally as a man with mortals and converses for a considerable time with men who entertain him unawares."[7] But this is no more supernatural than the inexplicable appearances of Jesus to his disciples when they were behind closed doors (Jn. 20: 19; 20: 26); and to call it a legend prejudices the case against its truthfulness. That the story possesses historical substance is suggested by the fact that this appearance occurred to two utterly insignificant disciples. The name of one is given as Cleopas (Lk. 24: 18), who is sometimes identified with the Clopas, Jesus' uncle (Jn. 19: 25). However, the two names are spelled differently, and there is no evidence to support the identification. The second disciple is altogether unnamed. If, as Luke records, the primary task of *apostles* was to bear witness to Jesus' resurrection (Acts 1: 22), we would expect that such an appearance would be to two of the apostles if the story is a community creation rather than to two unknown disciples who play no other role in the history of the early church.

That evening (apparently), Jesus appeared to the eleven who were gathered with other disciples (Lk. 24: 36ff). Then he led them out to Bethany outside of Jerusalem whence he parted from them to be taken up into heaven (Lk. 24: 50ff.).

It is clear that Luke is writing very selectively, for in his subsequent narrative he says that Jesus appeared to his disciples during a period of forty days (Acts 1: 3). Luke describes the ascension a second time giving considerably more detail than the Gospel. Again, Luke tells us that he appeared "for many days . . . to those who came up with him from Galilee to Jerusalem, who are now his witnesses to the people" (Acts 13: 31).

That Luke relates only appearances of Jesus in or near Jerusalem is easy to understand. The purpose of Acts is to show how the newborn church, which began as an unnoticed, insignificant group of Jewish believers in the capital city of Judaism, extended itself throughout the Roman world until it became a group of Gentile believers established in the very heart of the Roman empire. No other purpose can explain why Luke devotes amazingly large blocks of material — five and one half chapters (21: 17-26: 32) — to Paul's last experience in Jerusalem. No new churches were founded, no new teaching promulgated, no gains made by the church. Luke is concerned to relate at great length the fact that the natural people of God — Israel according to the flesh — as represented by the officials and the populace in the Holy City, rejected God's emissary in the person of Paul. Although rejected by Israel, not only in Jerusalem but also in Rome (Acts 28: 25-27), he found a hearing among the Gentiles; and Luke closes his book with the note of Paul's effective ministry among the Gentiles in Rome.[8]

Luke is not interested in writing a complete history nor does he have any particular interest in Galilee. He is interested in the movement from Jerusalem to Rome, and in connection with this interest, he relates only appearances in the neighbourhood of Jerusalem. Undoubtedly the command to the disciples not to leave Jerusalem (Acts 1: 4) was given after the disciples had returned from Galilee to Jerusalem.

The Fourth Gospel gives us appearances in both locales. John relates an appearance to Mary in Jerusalem, then two appearances to the disciples. In an appended chapter, Jesus revealed himself to the eleven by the sea of Galilee.

Thus Luke places the locale of the resurrection appearances only in Jerusalem; Mark places them (by implication) only in Galilee, while Matthew and Luke have Jesus revealing himself in both places. Many contemporary scholars feel that these two locales are mutually exclusive and that they must choose between them. The custom is to opt for Galilee. To illustrate: Hans von Campenhausen is one of Europe's most outstanding historians of the early church. In a widely influential essay on the resurrection, he outlines the events in this way. Immediately after Jesus' crucifixion, the disciples at first remained in Jerusalem but did not come into the open any more. They were bewildered and downcast, but "by no means resigned to what had happened". Very soon, probably on the third day, some woman discovered that the grave was open and empty. At this point, there were no appearances of Jesus. "The news caused unrest among the disciples. In particular, Peter seems to have understood the empty tomb as a pledge that the resurrection had occurred and to have influenced the others accordingly." Thereupon, the disciples departed to Galilee under the direction of Peter in hope of meeting Jesus there. In Galilee, Jesus appeared to Peter alone, then to the twelve, then to the five hundred brethren (1 Cor. 15), then to James, then to all the apostles. These appearances should be thought of as occurring in rapid succession. It is possible that the two latter appearances took place in Jerusalem. Only after the appearances in Galilee did the disciples return to Jerusalem.[9]

To this reconstruction, several objections must be raised. First, the gospels are unanimous that it was not the empty tomb that suggested the resurrection. Von Campenhausen appeals to Luke for support that Peter seems to have understood the empty tomb as a pledge that the resurrection had occurred and to have influenced the others accordingly. This is perplexing, for Peter is mentioned only once in Luke's account, when the two Emmaus disciples returned to Jerusalem to relate their meeting with Jesus. They were told, "The Lord has risen indeed, and has appeared to Simon" (Lk. 24: 34). *And this appearance must have occurred on Easter Sunday in Jerusalem.* To be sure, John relates that Peter and John visited the empty tomb and saw the grave clothes lying where Jesus' body had lain, and from the position of the grave clothes, "the other disciple . . . saw and believed" (Jn. 20: 8). (This incident will be dealt with below.) However, von Campenhausen appeals to Luke, not to John, to support his position. To be sure, there is a text in many manuscripts which is omitted from the R.S.V., N.E.B., and two of our three modern critical Greek texts. The Greek text published by the American Bible Society brackets this verse, because it "is regarded as having dubious textual validity". This verse reads, "But Peter rose and ran to the tomb; stooping and looking in, he saw the linen clothes by themselves; and he went home, wondering at what had happened" (Lk. 24: 12). This verse does not say that the empty tomb suggested the resurrection to Peter, only that it filled him with wonder. Paul refers to an appearance to Peter (1 Cor. 15: 5), but the only appearance to Peter in the Gospels alone is that referred to in Luke 24: 34, and this must have been in Jerusalem. In the case of John 20: 8 and Luke 24: 12, it was not the empty tomb that aroused faith in Peter but the linen clothes.

The empty tomb of itself did not create faith in the resurrection, neither on the part of Peter nor any of the other disciples. Mark records that not even the announcement of the angels that Jesus had arisen was believed. On the contrary, the women were filled with astonishment and fear (Mk. 16: 8). The two disciples on the Emmaus road had apparently heard that the tomb was empty but had not met anyone who had seen Jesus; and they were still filled with doubt (Lk. 24: 21). Luke records that when the women found the disciples and told them of finding the tomb empty, "these words seemed to them an idle tale, and they did not believe them" (Lk. 24: 11). *The empty tomb did not and does not arouse faith in the resurrection of Jesus.* It is a historical fact with which historical study of the resurrection must reckon, but historically it only witnesses that something happened to the body of Jesus; it does not suggest what happened. We must conclude that von Campenhausen goes beyond the evidence.

A second fact is important. According to the Gospels, the witness of the women was threefold: they found the tomb empty; an angel (or angels) announced that Jesus was risen; and they themselves saw Jesus, both the women (Mt. 28: 9-10) and Mary (Jn. 20). When they related their experiences to the disciples, they did not believe, for the women's words seemed to be an idle tale (Lk. 24: 11). This bears the marks of verisimilitude, for in the world of Judaism, there were no "liberated women". A woman had no right to bear witness, because it was concluded from Genesis 18: 15 that she was a liar. Only in a few very exceptional cases was her witness permissible.[10] In view of this fact, it is surely remarkable that the testimony of women both to the empty tomb and to the resurrection itself play so large a place in the Gospels. If the faith of the community had entered significantly into the substance of the resurrection stories, *we would have expected the primary witnesses to have been apostles* instead of women. The only intelligible reason for the primacy of the testimony of the women is that it is historically sound. There is therefore good critical reason for believing that the appearances took place both in Galilee and Jerusalem.[11]

In conclusion, it may be of some comfort to many readers to know that competent critical scholars accept both the Galilean and Jerusalem locales for the resurrection appearances. Probably England's greatest recent New Testament scholar was C. H. Dodd. In his last book, entitled *The Founder of Christianity*,[12] he has a brief chapter on the resurrection as the sequel to the life of Jesus, in which he writes as though he considered the appearances both in Galilee and Jerusalem to be true. C. F. D. Moule, in an essay on the ascension, suggests in passing that there is a case for both traditions.[13]

Is it possible to harmonise the divergent resurrection stories? Most modern critics throw up their hands and refuse to attempt any harmonisation. Indeed, they go further than to confess helplessness, to assert that the accounts are so contradictory that one must choose between several alternatives, eg., whether a group of women came to the tomb on Easter morning (synoptics), or whether Mary came alone. However its is possible that the several evangelists select their materials with a view to their own interests.

The gospels must be evaluated from the point of view of their *intention*, not from an artificial purpose superimposed upon them by a modern concept of historiography. It is clear that the Gospels *do not intend* to give us a complete record of all of the resurrection appearances. For instance, the account in Luke's gospel seems to have been compressed into a single day; but in opening the second volume of Luke-Acts, the author tells us that Jesus appeared to his disciples during a forty-day period (Acts 1: 3). John informs us that his gospel consists of only a selection of the many things Jesus did (Jn. 20: 30-31). Furthermore, Luke 24: 34 tells us that Jesus appeared to Peter, but none of the other gospels relates this appearance. In view of the leading role of Peter in the early church, this is an amazing omission. This appearance is confirmed by Paul's testimony to the resurrection in 1 Corinthians 15: 5. Furthermore, Paul tells us of an appearance to James the brother of Jesus, which is probably the occasion of his conversion, and of an appearance to five hundred brethren at one time, many of whom were still living to testify to their experience (1 Cor. 15: 6). It is clear that the evangelists have no intention of giving us a complete *history* of the resurrection appearances. They select incidents from the tradition known to them for one purpose: to establish the fact that Jesus, the crucified, was alive again.

Can the accounts be harmonised? The answer to that question depends on the stance of the critic. Some years ago, the present author, for his own amusement, undertook such a harmonisation, which has rested in his files for many years. He consulted no books but simply worked with the texts. In reading recent books on the resurrection, he found one scholar who also attempted a harmonisation, and to this writer's surprise, the two harmonisations are very similar to each other.[14] The major difference is that Perry thinks the appearance to the women recorded in Matthew 28: 9-10 is contradicted by Mark 16: 9: "He appeared first to Mary Magdalene." However, Mark 16: 9 is not a part of the authentic text and the appearance to the women is located neither temporally nor spacially.

For those who are interested in such a possible harmonisation, it is here included.

1. The earthquake and removal of stone occurs before dawn.

2. A group of four women come early to the tomb, wondering who will move the stone. As they approach, they are amazed to see that the stone has been rolled away.

3. Mary rushes off to tell Peter and John that the body of Jesus has been stolen (Jn. 20: 2).

4. The other women stay in the garden. They enter the tomb and are met by two angels, who tell them to carry word of the resurrection to the disciples. The problem of "a young man" of Mark 16: 5, "two men" of Luke 24: 4, "angels" of Luke 24: 23, is one of the "ordinary" Synoptic divergencies of detail.

5. The women rush away from the garden, filled with mingled emotions of fear and joy, speaking to no one about the vision of the angels at the empty tomb (Mk. 16: 8).

6. Later in the day, Jesus met them (Matthew 28: 9 does not say that this meeting occurred in the garden). They had run away from the tomb. Jesus tells them to bear the word to the disciples; they depart to find the disciples, who are not together but scattered (Mt. 26: 56).

7. Peter and John, having been informed by Mary, come to the tomb after the women have left. They see the clothes; vague comprehension dawns on John. They rush off to gather the disciples.

8. Mary returns to the tomb after Peter and John have left; they had run to the tomb (Jn. 20: 4), leaving Mary behind. She still thinks the body has been stolen. She is weeping outside the tomb, knowing nothing of the experience of the women she had left in the garden. She sees the two angels, then Jesus (Jn. 20: 11-17). (Mark 16: 9 is not authentic.)

9. After the first shock of amazement had worn off, the women find some of the disciples; the disciples cannot believe the fanciful story (Lk. 24: 11).

10. The disciples have gathered together.

11. Mary arrives and tells her experience (Jn. 20: 18).

12. That afternoon, the walk to Emmaus.

13. Sometime that afternoon, an appearance to Peter (Lk. 24: 34).

14. That evening, the disciples are all together in the closed room. They had been scattered, but the testimony of the women, of Peter and John, then of Mary, serves to bring them all together. Thomas was absent.

15. A second appearance to the eleven, including Thomas.
16. Galilee (Mt. 28: 16). The appearance by Tiberias (Jn. 21) and to the 500 brethren (1 Cor. 15: 6).
17. Return to Jerusalem; the final appearance and ascension.

This harmonisation does not mean that the author intends to suggest that the events actually happened in this order. We cannot know. As stated above, it is the purpose of no evangelist to give a complete history of the appearances. And even if the reader considers this harmonisation to be forced and artificial, this may in itself be a virtue. It is an amazing thing that none of the gospels reports the appearance to Peter (except Lk. 24: 34), to James, and to the five hundred (1 Cor. 15: 3-6). The most difficult single problem is the apparent flat contradiction between the appearance to the women in Matthew 28: 9-10 and the unqualified affirmation that "him they did not see" (Lk. 24: 24). However, as already pointed out, the appearance to the women is not located by way of time or place.

There may even be a virtue in the fact that the evangelists present such diverse accounts, for it shows their independence of each other and suggests that the points on which they do agree are likely to be all the more historically reliable.

The Gospels agree in certain important points which we may take as being historically credible.
1. Jesus was dead and buried.
2. The disciples were not prepared for his death; they were overcome with confusion.
3. The tomb was found on Easter morning to be empty.
4. The empty tomb was not itself a proof of the resurrection. Mary thought the body had been stolen.
5. The disciples encountered certain experiences which they took to be appearances of Jesus risen from the dead. In the last analysis, it does not really matter where or to whom these appearances occurred.
6. We must include another important historical fact. Contemporary Judaism had no concept of a dying and rising Messiah.
7. Another historical fact: the disciples proclaimed the resurrection of Jesus in Jerusalem, near where he had been buried.

The reader at this point will note that we have not committed ourselves to any view of the resurrection, but have simply attempted to spell out the solid, purely "historical" facts with which the historian must work.

There is one other bit of historical evidence which must be taken into account. When Mary informed Peter and John that the tomb was empty, the two of them ran to the tomb. In the tomb where the body of Jesus had lain, they "saw the linen clothes lying, and the napkin, which had been on his head, not lying with the linen clothes but rolled up in a place by itself" (Jn. 20: 7). As already noted, the body of Jesus had been wrapped in strips of cloth like a long bandage with spices placed between the several layers. The "napkin" was a separate piece of cloth which was wrapped over the head and under the chin to prevent the jaw from sagging. When Peter saw this he "believed" (Jn. 20: 8), namely, that Jesus was indeed risen from the dead. It was not the empty tomb which convinced him but the position in which the linen clothes lay. "It seems to be the evangelist's intention to suggest that Peter saw the grave clothes lying like a chrysalis out of which the risen body of the Lord had emerged."[15] This leads us for the first time to the question of the nature of the resurrection, as the Gospels represent it. It was not a revivification of a dead corpse, returning to physical life. Something happened to the body of Jesus, giving it new and marvellous powers. The body emerged from the grave clothes without disturbing them, leaving them intact. Obviously, Jesus had not *revived*. Obviously, the body had not been stolen. It had simply disappeared.

Is this a credible story? C. H. Dodd writes, "The story is told with the dramatic realism of which this writer is master. It looks like something as near first-hand evidence as we could hope to get. Perhaps it is, and if so, it becomes the sheet anchor of belief in a 'bodily' resurrection."[16] Therefore we are justified in concluding that the position of the grave clothes is another historical datum with which the historian must reckon.

One fact is of great importance: according to the testimony of our gospels, *no one witnessed the resurrection*. The texts in no way imply that the stone was rolled back from the tomb to let Jesus out; rather, the inference is that the stone was rolled back to let the disciples in. The earliest word of the angels is,

"He has risen, he is not here" (Mk. 16: 6). The experience that proved to the disciples the resurrection was not the empty tomb, nor even the word of the angels; it was their confrontation with the risen Jesus. They met him not in the act of rising from the dead but after he had risen. The gospel texts offer no explanation of the disciples' experience apart from the bare statement: "He has risen."

This remarkable restraint of our canonical gospels contrasts sharply with the apocryphal gospel of Peter.

Now in the night in which the Lord's day dawned, when the soldiers, two by two in every watch, were keeping guard, there rang out a loud voice in heaven, and they saw the heavens opened and two men come down from there in a great brightness and draw nigh to the sepulchre. That stone which had been laid against the entrance to the sepulchre started of itself to roll and gave way to the side, and the sepulchre was opened, and both the young men entered in. When now those soldiers saw this, they awakened the centurion and the elders for they also were there to assist at the watch. And whilst they were relating what they had seen, they saw three men come out of the sepulchre, and two of them sustaining the other, and a cross followed them, and the heads of the two reaching to heaven, but that of him who was led of them by the hand overpassing the heaven and they heard a voice out of the heavens saying, "Thou has preached to them that sleep." And from the cross there was heard the answer, "Yea." Those men took counsel with one another to go and report this to Pilate.[17]

Here is a vivid illustration of the difference between Gospel witness and legend. In the Gospel of Peter, the resurrection itself occurred during the last night (Saturday) before Easter morning, and it was witnessed by the guard and some of the elders of the Jews. In our gospels, at least in the resurrection stories, the actual resurrection is not located in time. As a matter of fact, we cannot say exactly when it occurred. The constant repetition of the idea of resurrection on the third day is probably due to the discovery of the empty tomb or the first appearances of the risen Lord on the third day.[18]

Here we stand face to face with mystery where speculation is of no avail. No one witnessed the resurrection, not even the most intimate disciples, much less those who were hostile to him. The fact of the matter is, as we shall see in detail later, the resurrection is not the return of Jesus to physical earthly life, but it is the event in which Jesus passed from earthly, mortal existence into the realm of immortality. This is the explanation of the grave clothes. The tomb was not opened to let Jesus out; he passed from the tomb while it was still closed. The grave clothes did not have to be stripped off to allow Jesus to emerge; he passed from the grave clothes while they still remained as they had been, rolled up around Jesus' body.

This is what throws the historian into despair. What does history—i.e., observed, open, human experience—know of restoration from death to life? But this is only half of the problem. What does history or nature or the totality of human experience know of any bodies which can pass through solid rock? This is *historically* incredible.

However, this interpretation does not rest merely upon the form of the grave clothes. There were other things about the risen Jesus that were marvellous. Both Luke and John record appearances which make it clear that Jesus, in his resurrection body, possessed unusual faculties. Luke (24: 13-53) tells the vivid story of two disciples who, on Sunday evening, were travelling from Jerusalem to Emmaus. They were not two of the eleven apostles. One was named Cleopas (vs. 18); the other remains unnamed. As they journeyed, Jesus drew near to them and began to walk along with them. However, Luke says that "their eyes were kept from recognising him" (vs. 16). One scholar thinks that this was due to the nature of Jesus' resurrection body. "Because Jesus' resurrection body was not so easily recognisable owing to its heavenly nature, the two disciples did not recognise him."[19] However, there is nothing in the Lukan account to suggest this. On the contrary, the language suggests that Jesus was recognisable, but the eyes of the two disciples were supernaturally veiled so that they did not recognise him. They told Jesus that they had heard stories about a visit of some women to the tomb, only to find it empty of Jesus' body. Angels told them that he was alive. They also told of the visit of certain disciples who found the tomb empty as the women had said, but they did not see Jesus. They gave voice to their former hope that Jesus was the Messiah—i.e., "that he was the one to redeem Israel" (vs. 21). The phrase "to redeem Israel" in this context does not refer to the redemption of men from their sins. In its present context, the phrase means to deliver Israel from her bondage to foreign powers. This same sentiment is expressed in Acts 1: 6 where Luke summarises the disciples' attitude by the question, "Lord, will you at this time restore the kingdom to Israel?" The disciples were still looking for a nationalistic and political saviour for the people of Israel, a hope which we have found in the apocalyptic literature.

Jesus rebuked them for failing to understand the prophetic scriptures; "And beginning with Moses and all the prophets, he interpreted to them in all the scriptures the things concerning himself" (vs. 27). Then as they drew near to Emmaus, the disciples, still in ignorance as to Jesus' identity, persuaded Jesus to stay with them and share their evening meal. As they sat at the table, he took bread and broke it and gave it to them. "And their eyes were opened and they recognised him; and he vanished out of their sight" (vs. 31). Reporting their experience to the eleven upon their return to Jerusalem, they told them what had happened, "and how he was known to them in the breaking of bread" (vs. 35). Many scholars have seen in these words an allusion to the institution of the Lord's Supper. This is attractive, but is rendered difficult by the fact that only the twelve were with Jesus in the upper room. We know it was Jesus' custom to return thanks before breaking bread (Mk. 6: 41), and it is possible that it was this act which disclosed his identity to the two disciples. However, the text expressly says, "And their eyes were opened and they recognised him" (vs. 31). This suggests only that the supernatural restraint was removed at the time Jesus broke bread.

This narrative says two things: the person of Jesus was capable of being recognised by those who had known him in his earthly ministry; and yet he was capable of sudden, inexplicable disappearance. Nothing like this ever happened "in the days of his flesh". Some scholars think that a supernatural disappearance is implied in the incident at Nazareth where the crowd tried to hurl Jesus headlong down a cliff

(Lk. 4: 30);[20] but this is not demanded by the text, which merely reads, "Passing through the midst of them, he went away" (Lk. 4: 30). Here is surely something marvellous: a real person in a real body who is recognisable, yet one who apparently can appear and disappear at will.

The same characteristics are evident in the next incident reported by Luke. As the two Emmaus disciples were relating their experience to the eleven, "Jesus himself stood among them" (Lk. 24: 36). In spite of the fact that he had already appeared to Peter (Lk. 24: 34), when Jesus suddenly and unexpectedly appeared out of nowhere in their midst, the disciples were startled and frightened, and "supposed that they saw a spirit" (Lk. 24: 37). It is not difficult to imagine their amazement. Suppose you, the reader, had attended the funeral of a friend, had seen the body in the casket, had seen the casket closed and lowered into the ground; and suppose three days later you suddenly came face to face with your friend; how would you react? I suspect most of us would conclude that our friend had an identical twin brother of whom we had never heard or seen. Little wonder that the disciples were hard to convince, and jumped to the initial conclusion that a spirit had appeared to them. Jesus assures them that it is he in person—indeed, in bodily form—by showing them his hands and feet; by bidding them to handle his body; by saying, "a spirit has not flesh and bones as you see that I have" (Lk. 24: 40). These words need not be taken to be a description of the actual material composition of Jesus' body, but are intended as a proof of Jesus' corporeity. One commentator says that this story is an account of "an appearance in the material body that had been buried in the sepulchre".[21] But a "material" body such as Jesus had before his crucifixion is incapable of suddenly materialising out of nowhere.

Then Jesus confirms the corporeity of his resurrection body by eating a piece of fish before the disciples. This again need be nothing more than evidence that Jesus' presence was in tangible, visible, bodily form.

The fourth Gospel records two incidents which are of the same order. On Sunday evening, the disciples were gathered together, "the doors being shut where the disciples were, for fear of the Jews" (Jn. 20: 19). This certainly means nothing less than that the doors were both shut and locked that no one might enter without warning. Nevertheless, suddenly Jesus came and stood among them. We may assume that at the end of this appearance, Jesus suddenly disappeared from sight as he had from the two disciples at Emmaus.

The same experience is repeated a week later. Again, the text explicitly says, "The doors were shut, but Jesus came and stood among them" (Jn. 20: 26). On this occasion, Jesus bade Thomas to feel his hands and his side to assure himself of the reality of the resurrection. Again, the text does not relate the nature of Jesus' disappearance. However, the purpose of these two stories is clear. It is to demonstrate that Jesus had a real, visible, palpable body, and yet a body which possessed new and marvellous properties. A recent commentator says that John's motive "was to suggest the mysterious power of the risen Jesus, who was at once sufficiently corporeal to show his wounds and sufficiently immaterial to pass through closed doors."[22] Yet it is not at all clear that this is precisely stated. There is no indication that Jesus actually passed through the closed door. All the text says, both in John and Luke, is that Jesus suddenly appeared and with equal suddenness disappeared. He possessed a real body, but also powers never before heard of—of being able to appear and disappear at will to the human physical senses.

These resurrection stories are in accord with what Paul tells us about the theology of the resurrection body—a subject to be treated at length in the next chapter. Jesus arose in a real body, but not in a natural, physical[23] body. Paul calls it a "spiritual body" (1 Cor. 15: 44). We may introduce this question by citing a modern historian whose reconstruction is more "critical" than that of the present author:

Here [in the resurrection] we are dealing with an event unique in every sense, with which the new "aeon" begins and in which, therefore, *the old world with its laws definitely ends* [italics ours]. Consequently, from the nature of the case, such an event is not to be assented to as merely "probable"; it must be seen as necessary and theologically "natural", as it were. The position is difficult only for those who would take the resurrection faith seriously, yet hold the bodily resurrection superfluous or unacceptable.[24]

We may conclude this chapter by asking what, according to the Gospel witness, actually happened at the moment of resurrection? The answer is that Jesus was raised from the realm of mortal men into the unseen world of God. *The resurrection appearances were not the resurrection itself.* They were momentary appearances of the invisible, risen Lord to the physical sight and senses of the disciples. Of course, if one chooses to believe that there is no divine, invisible world of God, or that the boundaries between the invisible and the visible worlds are inviolate, the resurrection stories are fantastic. But who can say that such a world does not exist? Who can say, for that matter, that God does not exist? Such questions are completely beyond the scope of the physical sciences and critical historiography.

We agree with Willi Marxsen that no one witnessed the resurrection, that the appearances are not identical with the resurrection itself, and that the belief in the resurrection is an inference drawn by the early disciples. Marxsen says it was an inference derived from personal faith.[25] However, this is to mis-state the facts. The belief in the resurrection was not an inference created by early Christian faith. On the contrary, we have seen that something had to happen to create faith in disheartened, unbelieving disciples. And, according to the witness of the gospels, that something was nothing less than appearances of the risen Jesus to the disciples. Faith did not beget faith. Bornkamm has seen this clearly. He states, "It is just as certain that the appearances of the risen Christ and the word of his witnesses have in the first place given rise to this faith."[26]

If the resurrection of Jesus was resurrection from the human, mortal world into the invisible, eternal world of God, the question remains, What actually happened at the moment of resurrection? What would an observer have seen if he had stood inside the tomb watching the dead body of Jesus? This must be speculation, but we believe it is based directly upon the witness of the gospels. All he would have seen was the sudden and inexplicable disappearance of the body of

Jesus. The grave clothes remained in the form in which they had been wrapped around Jesus. The tomb remained closed. But suddenly, Jesus' body disappeared. Jesus' dead body was raised into the immortal, eternal life of the world of God, which is invisible to mortal eyes, unless it makes itself visible. The appearances, then, were condescensions of the risen, exalted Lord by which he convinced his disciples that he was no longer dead.

If this reasoning is sound, it should become clear that witnessing the resurrection would of itself be no proof of the resurrection. It would be only a bewildering event which would leave the disciples in confusion, wondering what marvellous thing had happened. The appearances were necessary to convince the disciples that Jesus was really alive from the dead. The empty tomb did not prove this, as we have seen. The empty tomb was, however, a witness to the *nature* of the resurrection. It was not a "resurrection of Jesus' spirit," but a resurrection of his body. Neville Clark has well expressed it: ". . . the empty tomb stands as the massive sign that the eschatological deed of God is not outside this world of time and space or in despair of it, but has laid hold on it, penetrated deep into it, shattered it, and begun its transformation."[27]

This is why many modern scholars who believe in the eventfulness, the facticity, and the "objectivity" of the resurrection—in the sense that it was a real event that actually happened *in history*, outside of me and outside of all human experience—have difficulty with the "historicity" of the resurrection. It was an event that was observed by no one, an event caused by God—indeed, an event in which the world of God intersected the world of time and space. Thus Bornkamm is correct in saying,

> What became clear and grew to be a certainty for the church was this, that God himself had intervened with his almighty hand in the wicked and rebellious life of the world and had wrested this Jesus of Nazareth from the power of sin and death which had risen against him, and set him up as Lord of the world.[28]

The problem is, how can a historian *as historian* talk about the world of God, or the acts of God, even if they occurred in history? All the historian as such can say is that something marvellous has happened here. *Only those who have reason to believe in the God to whom the Bible witnesses can accept the witness of the gospels, viz., that God raised Jesus from the dead.*

NOTES

1. Reginald H. Fuller, *The Formation of the Resurrection Narratives* (New York: Macmillan, 1971), p. 2.
2. See G. E. Ladd, *The New Testament and Criticism* (London/Grand Rapids: Hodder & Stoughton and Eerdmans, 1967), pp. 123ff.
3. C. E. B. Cranfield, *The Gospel according to Saint Mark* (Cambridge: University Press, 1959), p. 464.
4. A. Edersheim, *The Life and Times of Jesus the Messiah* (New York: Longmans, Green, 1896), II, p. 618.
5. Michael C. Perry, *The Easter Enigma* (London: Faber and Faber, 1959), p. 66.
6. C. E. B. Cranfield, *op. cit.*, p. 469.
7. C. F. Evans, *Resurrection and the New Testament* (Naperville: Allenson, 1970), p. 105.
8. See G. E. Ladd, *The Young Church* (London/Nashville: Lutterworth and Abingdon, 1964).
9. Hans von Campenhausen, "The Events of Easter and the Empty Tomb," *Tradition and Life in the Church* (Philadelphia: Fortress, 1968), pp. 85f.
10. J. Jeremias, *Jerusalem in the Time of Jesus* (Philadelphia: Fortress, 1969), p. 374.
11. "The Christian claim that the women found the tomb empty has not really been proved to be of late origin; rather, such a claim may have been presupposed as far back as we can trace the tradition of the proclamation that Jesus had been raised." R. E. Brown, *The Gospel according to St. John* (Garden City: Doubleday, 1970), II, p. 928. See also C. F. D. Moule, *The Significance of the Message of the Resurrection for Faith in Jesus Christ*, ed. by C. F. D. Moule (London/Naperville: S.C.M. & Allenson, 1968), p. 9.
12. New York/London: Macmillan, 1970.
13. See *The Expository Times* 68 (1956–7), p. 207.
14. See Michael C. Perry, *The Easter Enigma* (London: Faber and Faber, 1959), pp. 65, 70.
15. S. H. Hooke, *The Resurrection of Christ* (London: Darton, Longman and Todd, 1967), p. 79.
16. C. H. Dodd, *The Founder of Christianity* (London: Macmillan, 1970), p. 164.
17. *The Gospel of Peter*, pp. 35–43.

18. See G. Delling in Kittel's *Theological Dictionary of the New Testament* (Grand Rapids: Eerdmans, 1972), VIII, p. 220.

19. N. Geldenhuys, *Commentary on the Gospel of Luke* (Grand Rapids: Eerdmans, 1950), p. 632.

20. See J. M. Creed, *The Gospel according to St. Luke* (London: Macmillan, 1930), p. 69.

21. S. M. Gilmour in *The Interpreter's Bible* (New York: Abingdon-Cokesbury, 1952), 8, p. 430.

22. C. K. Barrett, *The Gospel according to St. John* (London: S.P.C.K., 1955), p. 472.

23. We use the word "physical" to designate the same kind of body as our present bodies of weak mortal flesh and blood.

24. Hans von Campenhausen, *op. cit.*, pp. 86f.

25. Willi Marxsen, *The Resurrection of Jesus of Nazareth* (Philadelphia: Fortress, 1970), p. 138.

26. Günther Bornkamm, *Jesus of Nazareth* (New York: Harper, 1960), p. 183.

27. As quoted by C. F. D. Moule, *op. cit.*, p. 7. This book is unavailable to me.

28. G. Bornkamm, *loc. cit.*

CHAPTER 9

The Witness of Paul

WE HAVE CONSIDERED at considerable length the witness of the Gospels to the resurrection of Jesus. It is time to turn now to the witness of Paul. Paul preserves for us the earliest tradition of the resurrection appearances of Jesus. We have mentioned that the Gospels were written at least a generation after the events they record, and the tradition of these events was preserved in oral form before it was written down by the evangelists. Paul gives us an earlier tradition. Writing to the Corinthians about A.D. 55 or 56, Paul says:

> For I delivered to you as of first importance what I also received, that Christ died for our sins in accordance with the scriptures, that he was buried, that he was raised on the third day in accordance with the scriptures, and that he appeared to Cephas, then to the twelve. Then he appeared to more than five hundred brethren at one time, most of whom are still alive though some have fallen asleep. Then he appeared to James, then to all the apostles. Last of all, as to one untimely born, he appeared also to me. (1 Cor. 15: 3-8).

This is the most striking and important account of the resurrection appearances in the New Testament. In saying that he *delivered* to the Corinthians what he *received*, he is using the customary idiom that denotes receiving and handing on oral tradition. Paul affirms that the Gospel message did not originate with him, but he received it from others to whom it had been committed before him. It is widely admitted that Paul is probably referring to his visit to Jerusalem described in Galatians 1:18 three years after his conversion. To be sure, Paul elsewhere claims not to have received his Gospel from men or through any human mediator but from the Lord alone (Gal. 1:12). By this, Paul means to say that his message about Jesus as the exalted Lord came to him by direct revelation on the Damascus road when Christ appeared to him; but this by no means precludes the probability that when Paul visited Jerusalem shortly after his conversion, he met and talked with Peter and James, and learned from them the important facts about Jesus' life, death, and resurrection appearances. If this is so, this tradition about the resurrection appearances of Jesus goes back to a point only ten years or so later than the events it relates. This has led the Heidelberg historian, von Campenhausen, to say, "This account meets all the demands of historical reliability that could possibly be made of such a text as things stood."[1]

It is of great interest to note how this account differs from the witness of the Synoptic Gospels. It is obvious that Paul embodies an independent tradition. The appearance to Cephas, whose person was influential in the Corinthian church (1 Cor. 1:12), is not mentioned in the Synoptics, except in the passing reference in Luke 24:34, and as we have already indicated, this appearance, according to Luke, happened on Easter Sunday in Jerusalem. The appearance "to the twelve" could either be the appearance to the eleven recorded in Luke 24:36-49, or one of the appearances in John 20. The appearance to five hundred brethren at one time is most impressive and is a valuable datum in trying to decide what is the nature of the appearances. It would seem most likely that this appearance occurred in Galilee where Jesus had spent most of his ministry. It is indeed a powerful witness when Paul says that most of the witnesses are still alive and therefore, presumably, can be questioned about their experience. We know absolutely nothing about the appearance to James — either when or where it occurred. It is highly probable that it was this experience which made James a believer. "In the days of his flesh," Jesus' family did not understand him and were not counted among his followers (Mk. 3:21, 31; Jn. 7:5).

In the earliest days of the primitive church while it was largely limited to Jerusalem, Peter and John were the foremost leaders (Acts 3: 1; 4: 13; 8: 14). However, after the church began to scatter outside of Jerusalem, James the brother of Jesus suddenly emerges as the central figure in the Jerusalem community (Acts 12: 17; see also Gal. 1: 19; 2: 9) and James appears to be the dominating figure at the council in Jerusalem (Acts 15: 13). When Paul made his last visit to Jerusalem, James is clearly the representative head of the church (Acts 21: 18), whatever official or unofficial capacity he may have occupied. In later Christian tradition James was the first bishop of the church in Jerusalem.[2] Paul includes James in the category of apostles (Gal. 2: 19).

The statement that Jesus appeared to "all the apostles" is difficult. It may designate an appearance to the eleven, plus James, whom Paul considered an apostle.[3] If so, this is an appearance which is not recorded in the gospels.

Paul includes the appearance to himself to be on a par with that of all the others. "Last of all, . . . he appeared also to me."

Before we consider the meaning of this statement, we must consider a prior question. Why does Paul go out of his way to say that Jesus was buried? Of course, dead men are always buried. The reason for this statement is vigorously debated in the contemporary literature. Some think that Paul affirms the burial to confirm the reality of Jesus' death. This however seems unnecessary. As already stated, dead men are always buried. Many scholars see here an oblique reference to the empty tomb. It was the entombed *body* of Jesus that was raised from the dead, leaving the tomb empty.[4] However, in the Pauline context, this is not an important point, for, as we shall see, Paul knows of no resurrection except a bodily one.

A further question is raised by Paul's statement that "he was raised on the third day in accordance with the scriptures" (vs. 4). This reminds us of the incident on the Emmaus road when Jesus, "beginning with Moses and all the prophets, . . . interpreted to them in all the scriptures the things concerning himself" (Lk. 24: 27), especially with reference to the fact that "the Christ should suffer these things and enter into his glory" (vs. 26). From our modern point of view, these are difficult sayings. We have already thoroughly canvassed the Old

Testament data and have discovered that it does not predict a suffering *Messiah.*[5] It does relate the sufferings of an unnamed servant of the Lord, but he is not the Messiah. Messiah, according to such passages as Psalm 2, Isaiah 9 and 11 is a victorious, conquering Davidic king, not a humble servant who pours out his soul in sufferings and death. However, here is a fundamental Biblical hermeneutic. The New Testament writers do not interpret the Old Testament by the historical method like a modern scholar does. *They interpreted it in light of Christ.* New and deeper—and even previously unseen meanings were found in the sacred text. Thus Isaiah 53 becomes a prophecy of the suffering Messiah. This is clearly proven by Philip's experience with the Ethiopian eunuch (Acts 8: 27-35).

This may be again illustrated by Luke's report of Peter's first sermon in Acts. In support of the resurrection, Peter quotes the word of Psalm 16, "Moreover my flesh will dwell in hope. For thou wilt not abandon my soul to Hades, nor let the Holy One see corruption" (Acts 2: 26f.). Peter finds in these words God's promise that it was impossible for Jesus the Messiah to be held in bondage by death. However, we have already seen that in its own context, this is a promise of the hope of deliverance from Sheol after death, not of resurrection from the dead.[6]

An even more radical interpretation occurs in the same sermon with reference to the exaltation of Jesus. Again, Peter quotes from Psalm 110, "The Lord [Jahweh] said to my Lord [the King], Sit at my right hand, till I make thy enemies a stool for thy feet." In its Old Testament setting, this is a promise of the enthronement of David's son on the king's throne in Jerusalem. The second verse says, "The Lord sends forth *from Zion* your mighty sceptre. Rule in the midst of your foes!" A reference in 1 Chronicles 29: 23 proves that the king's throne in Jerusalem can be called the Lord's throne. "Then Solomon sat on the throne of the Lord as king instead of David." The Psalm predicts the enthronement of David's son on the throne of Israel—and of God—in Jerusalem. Peter, under divine inspiration, sees here a prophecy of the enthronement of the ascended Lord at the right hand of God. *Peter deliberately transfers the throne from Jerusalem to heaven.* This is a principle of biblical interpretation which can be illustrated innumerable times. Early Christian faith reinterpreted the Old Testament in the light of the new revelatory events in Christ. This does not mean necessarily a one-to-one relationship of prophecy and fulfilment. It means that the entire movement of Old Testament history and prophecy finds its fulfilment in Christ.

The question remains: What specific scriptures could Paul have had in mind when he says that Christ was raised on the third day "in accordance with the scriptures"? The clearest possible reference is to Hosea 6: 2: "After two days he will revive us; on the third day he will raise us up that we may live before him." In their Old Testament context, these words express the hope of a speedy restoration from national death in captivity.[7] However, this passage was quoted by Jewish rabbis to give Old Testament proof of the eschatological resurrection of God's people,[8] and it is possible that this passage was in Paul's mind.

We also recall Jesus' words; "For as Jonah was three days and three nights in the belly of the whale, so will the son of man be three days and nights in the heart of the earth" (Mt. 12: 40). We cannot be certain as to what specific texts, if any, Paul had in mind. He may have had in mind the frequency with which "three" appears in the Old Testament.[9] We cannot know.

The quotation from Matthew raises another problem. Paul says that Jesus was raised on the third day. The citation in Matthew 12: 40 says that the Son of Man will be three days and three nights in the heart of the earth—i.e., in the tomb. Scholars usually conclude that Jesus was crucified on Friday, was in the tomb Friday night, all day Saturday and Saturday night and rose on Sunday morning. In other words, he was in the tomb two nights and one day, not three days and three nights. A few students have tried to argue that Jesus must have been crucified on Thursday in the effort to harmonise chronology with Matthew 12: 40. However, Jesus is also reported to have said, "on the third day". The Synoptic writers felt no embarrassment at these two forms of expression. Both Matthew (12: 40; 27: 63) and Mark (10: 34) report the saying about resurrection "after three days"; but both of them

(Mt. 16: 21; 17: 23; and Lk. 9: 22) have "on the third day". Matthew (16: 21) and Luke (9: 22) feel free to change Mark's "after three days" (Mk. 8: 31) to "on the third day". Students of the Greek language have proven that, contrary to English usage, the two phrases were identical in meaning.[10]

A further consideration faces us at this point. If our argument is sound that no one saw Jesus actually rise from the dead — indeed, the nature of the event was such that no one could see it — how did the tradition come into being that he rose on the third day? The answer to this question is forthright: "In primitive Christianity the number three derives from the Easter tradition in which the day of the resurrection is the same as that of the discovery of the empty tomb or the first appearances of the Risen Lord."[11]

The most important phrase in this passage is the last one, "Last of all, he appeared also to me" (vs. 8). We must note once again that Paul classes his meeting with the risen Lord on the same level and of the same kind as the earlier appearances to the disciples. Furthermore, this is the "last" appearance. Apparently Paul knows of no other appearances of Jesus. With his experience, they ceased.

Furthermore, there is something unnatural about the appearance to Paul. It occurred "as to one untimely born". This translation does not bring out the exact meaning of the Greek word: *ektrōma*, which means literally a premature birth, such as an abortion or miscarriage. The word never means a delayed birth, which is the required meaning in this passage. However, the precise meaning of the word need not be pressed; it can be taken in a general way to indicate simply that Paul was not born spiritually at the right time, since he had not been a disciple during the lifetime of Jesus. The appearance of the risen Christ which both brought him into the Christian life and brought to him his call as an apostle did not occur in the normal orderly sequence. "The main emphasis is on the abnormality of the process, which took place when the Risen Lord had ceased to manifest himself to the disciples."[12]

Paul's personal testimony about the appearance of the risen Jesus has been used in two very different ways. On the one hand, it has been argued that Paul's experience on the

Damascus Road was a visionary sort of experience, which embodied primarily the phenomenon of light, and we must assume that all of the appearances after the resurrection were of the same sort. The record in our gospels has objectified this experience so that the precise form of the resurrection stories is not historically reliable. These were all extraordinary visions not seen by everyone.[13] Pannenberg does indeed go to considerable lengths to argue that the "subjective vision" theory is no longer tenable. What the disciples saw was not something in their own heads; it was a reality outside of themselves. Pannenberg goes on to suggest that the modern study of parapsychology has reopened the question of the reality of such objective visions.

On the other hand, the form of Paul's expression has been used to argue that Paul is defending the complete objectivity of his experience. "If Paul uses the same language of his own experience as of the experience of Peter and the others, it is to suggest not that their experience was as visionary as his but that his was as objective as theirs."[14]

This division of opinion makes it mandatory that we survey in detail what can be known about the Damascus Road experience. The most important fact is that Paul himself affirms vigorously that he has seen Jesus after his resurrection. In Galatians 1: 16, Paul describes the appearance of Christ as a revelation of his son "to me" (R.S.V.). The Greek has the preposition *en* meaning *in*. Some have tried to argue from this language that Paul means to say that he received an entirely inward, subjective revelation. However, our best Greek philology does not sustain that position; " . . . speculations on the inwardness of the Damascus experience have no philological basis."[15] The preposition *en* may be used to express the simple dative.

In another setting, Paul makes the unqualified affirmation that he has seen the Risen Lord. "Am I not free? Am I not an apostle? Have I not seen Jesus our Lord?" (1 Cor. 9: 1). The form of this statement suggests that Paul had in mind the fact that in the early church only those who had actually witnessed the resurrected Lord could be recognised as apostles (Acts 1: 22). This would seem to be the qualification which equipped James to be an apostle (Gal. 1: 19). James, like

Paul, had seen the risen Lord. That Paul classes the appearance of Jesus to him with the appearances to the other disciples suggests that "this presence [of the risen Christ] is in non-visionary reality; no category of human seeing is wholly adequate for it."[16]

Elsewhere Paul speaks of "visions and revelations of the Lord" (2 Cor. 12:1) which were frequently given to him. He selects one single experience which occurred to him "fourteen years ago" when in ecstasy he was caught up to the very presence of God "and heard things that cannot be told, which man may not utter" (1 Cor. 12:4). He describes his ecstatic experience by saying that he does not know whether he was in the body or out of the body. However, it is clear that Paul does not class his Damascus Road experience together with these ecstatic visions. The use of the plural form of the nouns in 1 Corinthians 12:1 "necessarily refers to experiences of a different kind from the Damascus experience".[17] On the Damascus Road, Paul is convinced that he came face to face with Jesus, now risen from the dead and exalted; and this confrontation completely changed the course of his life.

We come now to the most important and difficult question in Paul's thought. How does Paul conceive of the resurrected Christ? In what form does he exist? The answer to these questions is clear, and yet mind-staggering. It is clear that Paul conceives of resurrection as a *bodily* resurrection, and yet it will be a *glorified* body, which belongs to the *Age to Come*. Each of these three positions demands careful treatment.

For many modern Christians, the question of the "last things" or eschatology is little more than an appendix to their theology, not an integral part of it. Many Christians are essentially Greek in their view of the future. Final salvation occurs when we die and go to heaven to be with the Lord. Now it is true that Paul conceives of an intermediate state for believers when their spirits have left their bodies and are with the Lord. He speaks of this hope in two places. Writing to the Corinthians, Paul says, "We know that while we are at home in the body we are away from the Lord, for we walk by faith, not by sight. We are of good courage, and we would rather be away from the body and at home with the Lord" (2 Cor. 5:6-8). This is all Paul says. He does not say where this is: it is with the Lord. He says nothing about the condition of the dead in Christ or what kind of existence they have. In verse 3, he speaks of it as "nakedness", i.e., the state of being a disembodied spirit. This however is only a temporary condition. What Paul longs for is to receive "a building from God, a house not made with hands, eternal in the heavens" (2 Cor. 5: 1) so that "what is mortal may be swallowed up in life" (2 Cor. 5: 4). It is true that some scholars find in this passage a reference to a body which is put on by the believer at death,[18] but this interpretation is beset by unnecessary difficulties. In this passage, Paul says little more than he says in Philippians 1: 22-24: "Yet which I shall choose I cannot tell. I am hard pressed between the two. My desire is to depart and be with Christ, for that is far better. But to remain in the flesh is more necessary on your account." To depart and be with Christ: this is all that Paul says about the intermediate state. In fact, Paul says little more than do some of the Psalmists in their hope for deliverance from Sheol. The major difference is to depart and be *with Christ*, the resurrected Lord.

It is clear that for Paul, the goal of individual salvation is the resurrection which will occur at the Parousia, or coming of Christ, not only to raise the dead but also to inaugurate the Age to Come. Paul, like our Lord,[19] views the sweep of redemptive history not only in terms of heaven above and earth below, but in terms of two ages: this age and the Age to Come (see Eph. 1: 21). Oscar Cullmann is the modern scholar who has laid emphasis upon this eschatological structure of New Testament theology.[20] This age, which extends from creation to the Parousia, is called "this present evil age" (Gal. 1: 4) from whose powers men need to be delivered. Satan is called the "god of this age" (2 Cor. 4: 4). In his sovereign wisdom God has allowed the powers of evil to exercise such dominance in this age that Satan is called its god. However, the powers of Satan are always limited by the will and power of God. In his death and resurrection, Christ has rendered the rule of Satan a radical defeat.[21] In his resurrection and ascension, Christ has been enthroned at the right hand of God, and exalted above the evil powers of this age (Eph. 1: 20-21). God has given him the name that is above every name—Lord (Phil. 2: 11); and before the lordship of Christ,

every creature must bow in obedient confession, whether
human or superhuman creatures (Phil. 2: 10). In his exaltation,
Christ has been seated at the right hand of God where he has
begun his reign as messianic Lord. He is to reign until he has
put all his enemies under his feet; and the last enemy to be
destroyed is death (1 Cor. 15: 24-26). Here is the goal of
redemption: the divine order re-established in the whole of
God's creation, when all evil powers—sin, Satan, and death—
will be abolished. God's plan is to reunite all things in Christ,
both in the visible and the invisible world (Eph. 1: 10).

Paul says little about the state of affairs in the Age to Come
when Christ has finally abolished all enemies. He does, however, make it clear that redemption includes the physical
creation. "Creation itself will be set free from its bondage to
decay and obtain the glorious liberty of the children of God"
(Rom. 8: 21). Who can conceive of such a state of affairs—a
world in which flowers do not die, strong animals do not prey
upon the weak, earthquakes, storms and tornadoes no longer
wreak havoc and destruction? This however is the uniform
biblical theology; and the New Testament hope is essentially
no less earthly than the Old Testament hope.[22] This is why
biblical scholars speak of this new redeemed order of life as
lying *beyond history*. It will embody a quality of life such as
history has never seen, and which it is difficult to imagine—
life no longer determined by the so-called laws of nature,
struggle for survival, survival of the fittest, and the rule of
decay and death. Who can grasp what it means to live in a
world entirely freed from corruption, decay, deterioration and
death? It is an elemental truth of biology that death is a
necessary element in the on-going cycle of nature. The strong
constantly prey upon the weak. The cycle of the seasons is a
cycle of life and death. Clearly, history knows nothing of such
immortal existence. Life in a world freed from corruption
means nothing less than a complete transformation of human,
historical existence as it has been known on this planet for
millennia.

While Paul says very little about the state of affairs for the
world in the Age to Come, he says a great deal about individual
existence. He describes this in terms of the resurrection of the
body. His teaching about resurrection had been challenged in

Corinth, and this leads him to devote a long chapter to the nature of the resurrection. This gives us great insight into his thought and yet leaves us with intriguing but unsolvable problems. It is not altogether clear precisely what point of view the apostle is opposing. There may have been some in the Corinthian church who could not conceive of any kind of life after death. It is also possible that he was confronted with certain teachers who held that the resurrection was already past, in which case it would be a "spiritual" and not bodily resurrection. He had to face such a teaching when he wrote Second Timothy (see 2 Tim. 2: 18). It is more probable that he faced the teaching of a Greek dualism which accepted the immortality of the spirit after the death of the body but denied any resurrection of the body.

In refuting this false teaching, Paul links together inseparably the resurrection of Christ and the resurrection of believers at the end of the age. If Christ has not been raised, all else is false (vv. 12-19. This will be considered later). He says two things about the resurrection of believers: Theirs will be a resurrection of the *body*, but of a *transformed* body.

He faces the question, "How are the dead raised? With what kind of body do they come?" (vs. 35). We should recall here certain prominent Jewish teachings about resurrection which held either that the resurrection body will be identical with the mortal earthly body (2 Macc. 14: 46; see p. 56) or that the same earthly body would be raised and only later transformed (Apoc. Bar. 50: 2; see p. 57). Paul's first answer is that the resurrection will be a resurrection of the *body*. To establish this, he uses a rather imperfect metaphor: that of sowing a naked seed which dies but from which comes forth a new body (vv. 35-38). That the analogy is imperfect is seen from the fact that in agriculture, the bare kernel planted in the ground carries within itself the power of germination so that death is not the final word; life is perpetuated. But who can find in the realm of nature adequate analogies for supernatural truth? The resurrection is an *act of God*, not a process of nature. Yet to the observer, it is a marvellous thing that a dried-up, dead-looking seed of corn is buried in the ground only to have a beautiful green blade spring forth. After all, Jesus used the parable of seeds of grain (Mk. 4: 26-29) to teach the contrast between the present and future aspects of the Kingdom which is altogether God's deed, not a process of nature.[23] The point is that one body is buried in the ground; another *body* springs forth. That this is Paul's meaning is proven by his statement, "But God gives it a body as he has chosen, and to each kind of seed its own body" (vs. 38).

Then Paul goes on to say that the resurrection body will be different from the mortal body. He begins by saying that not all flesh is alike. There is one kind of flesh for men, another for animals, another for birds, another for fish (vs. 39). Paul is here using the word flesh as synonymous with the word body. Later on, Paul asserts that "flesh and blood cannot inherit the kingdom of God" (vs. 50), that is, our present earthly, mortal, decaying bodies cannot inherit the glorious world of immortal existence. The perishable cannot inherit the imperishable (vs. 50). It would perhaps be too much to read into Paul's words, "there is one flesh for mortal man, there is another flesh for the immortal resurrection." But the least that Paul means is that there is a mortal *body* and there is an immortal *body*.

He illustrates this further by saying, "there are celestial bodies and there are terrestrial bodies; but the glory of the celestial is one, and the glory of the terrestrial is another. There is one glory of the sun, and another glory of the moon, and another glory of the stars; for star differs from star in glory" (vv. 40-41). The heavens by day and night prove that there are many different bodies which differ from each other in glory.

These illustrations from nature and astronomy do not *prove* the resurrection but illustrate that there can be a *body* in the resurrection which is different from the mortal body that is buried. Then Paul comes as close as any New Testament writer to a description of the resurrection body. But he completely fails to describe the composition or matter of the body, he contents himself with some of its characteristics. The mortal body is perishable, dishonouring and weak; the resurrection body will be imperishable, glorious, and powerful (vv. 42-43). Who can imagine a body without weakness? or infection? or tiredness? or sickness? or death? This is a body, utterly unknown to earthly, historical existence. What Paul says about the body is parallel to what he says about the deliverance of creation from its bondage to decay. Salvation means the salvation of the *whole man*, not merely of his soul or spirit. Here Paul is at one with the Old Testament view of man.[24] In biblical thought, earthly bodily existence in itself is good. It is an evil only because "creation was subjected to futility" (Rom. 8: 20) because of man's sin. Therefore when redemption is complete, the whole creation—the whole man will be redeemed. Everywhere in the Bible, the ultimate destiny of man is a redeemed, transfigured earth, dwelling in redeemed, transfigured bodies.

Paul sums up his argument by saying, "It is sown a physical body, it is raised a spiritual body" (vs. 44). These words are subject to misinterpretation and taken to mean that the resurrection will be in "spiritual", i.e. non-corporeal bodies. This cannot be Paul's meaning. The translation "physical body" is not accurate; as a matter of fact, the Greek word has no equivalent term in English. The Greek word is *psychikon*, from *psyche* which means life or soul. The physical—i.e., mortal—body is not made of *psyche*; it is a body animated by *psyche*. In the same way the resurrection body will not be made of *pneuma*—spirit. It is true that some Greek philosophers did not consider *pneuma* to be non-material as we do; they thought of *pneuma* as a very fine, invisible, celestial substance capable of interpenetrating all other forms of being. However, this idea is not found in Paul. *Pneuma* to him is God's pneuma—the Holy Spirit. The resurrection body will be one which is completely animated and empowered by the Spirit of God.

It is true that Paul conceives of God's *pneuma* as dwelling in believers here and now; but the sphere of the Spirit's work in this life is the human spirit, not the human body. When Paul tells the Ephesians that they once were dead but now have been made alive, he refers to spiritual life. In spirit, we have been made alive with Christ. In spirit, we have been raised up with him. In spirit, we have even been exalted to heaven and seated at the right hand of God with Christ (Eph. 2: 5-6). Again Paul says, "But if Christ is in you, although your bodies are dead because of sin, your spirits are alive because of righteousness" (Rom. 8: 10). In the next verse, Paul makes it clear that to have Christ dwelling in one is identical to having the Spirit indwell one. Thus Paul can say that we have this treasure of the knowledge of the glory of God in the face of Christ in earthen vessels (2 Cor. 4: 7) which are subject to all kinds of sufferings.

Thus the *pneumatikon sōma* is a body transformed by the life-giving Spirit of God adapted for existence in the new redeemed order of the Age to Come. If scholars feel obliged to say that such existence is "beyond history", they do not mean to say that it is unreal or non-existent; they only mean to say it is an order of existence in which the "laws of nature" and normal historical causality no longer obtain. In fact, when one puts his mind to it, it is quite unimaginable.

Corresponding to this is a word from the Lord recorded in Luke 20: 34-36: "The sons of this age marry and are given in marriage; but those who are accounted worthy to attain to that age [i.e., the Age to Come] and to the resurrection from the dead neither marry nor are given in marriage, for they cannot die any more, because they are equal to angels and are sons of God, being sons of the resurrection." Historical existence in every culture is based in one way or another on the sex drive — family, parents, children, husbands, wives. Who can imagine existence in which these basic sociological and emotional and physical facts no longer prevail? Such is truly unimaginable.

Paul then adds a word very difficult to understand. "The first man Adam became a living being; the last Adam became a life-giving spirit" (vs. 45). In these words Paul contrasts the two heads of two different families: the family of Adam consisting of all men; and the family of Christ consisting of all believers, who are therefore indwelt by the Spirit and who find their existence "in Christ". The word describing Adam is literally "a living soul" (*psyche*). Adam's existence was altogether on the level of *psyche* — natural, human life. As such, Adam — and all the children of Adam — have "natural" (*psychika*) bodies. Christ in his resurrection entered into a new realm of existence — a new order, which is nothing less than the invisible world of God — the Age to Come. As such Paul calls him "a life-giving Spirit". He has entered the spiritual realm, taking his resurrected, glorified body with him.

In other places, Paul expresses the same truth. A much-debated verse is 2 Corinthians 3: 17: "Now the Lord is the

Spirit, and where the Spirit of the Lord is, there is freedom."
At first glance, these words seem to identify the risen Lord and
the Holy Spirit; but this cannot be Paul's intent, as the last
words show. Paul seems to identify the Lord and the Spirit,
and yet at the same time to distinguish between them. This
strange phenomenon appears in numerous places in other
idioms. Thus there is no difference between being indwelt by
Christ or by his Spirit (Rom. 8: 9-11). There is no distinct
difference between being in Christ and being in the Spirit.
To be "in the Spirit" means to be indwelt by the new life that
is in Christ (Rom. 8: 9). The same is true of being "in Christ"
(2 Cor. 5: 17). Such verses do not mean that Christ and the
Spirit are actually identical, for in 2 Corinthians 3: 17b, Paul
clearly differentiates between them by speaking of "the Spirit
of the Lord". However, since Christ entered the realm of the
Spirit at his resurrection, functionally and dynamically the
Lord and the Spirit are one. The exalted Lord works in the
world and within his people through the Spirit.

In the passage in First Corinthians, Paul goes on to speak of
the two families in Adam and in Christ. When he contrasts the
first man who came from the earth with the second man who
comes from heaven (vs. 47), he must be referring to the
Parousia of Christ, for Christ in his incarnation was also a
son of Adam in that he bore a "natural" mortal body. Just as
we have borne the image of the man of dust by being born in
corruptible, dying bodies, we shall also bear the image of the
man from heaven (vs. 49) at his Parousia. Paul says the same
thing in different words in Philippians 3: 21 when, speaking
of the return of the Lord, he says that the Lord "will change
our lowly body to be like his glorious body, by the power which
enables him even to subject all things to himself." Here, in a
letter written after the Corinthian correspondence, Paul clearly
affirms that the risen Lord exists in a body; but it is a glorious
body; and believers will one day share his glory, even in the
bodily mode of existence. Truly, this is life in the Age to Come,
beyond "history".

The mention of "glory" brings to mind a whole series of
references which have a strong emphasis upon eschatology or
the consummation of God's redemptive purpose. Sharing God's
glory is one of the most frequently repeated idioms used to

describe the final destiny of the redeemed. This goes back to the
Old Testament. The coming of God's Kingdom means that
"they shall see the glory of the Lord" (Isa. 35: 2). "I am
coming to gather all nations and tongues; and they shall come
and shall see my glory" (Isa. 66: 18). This theme is even more
often repeated in the New Testament, where "glory" comes
to be the sum and substance of the eschatological expectation.
"Where Christ who is our life appears, then you will appear
with him in glory" (Col. 3: 4). "Christ in you, the hope of
glory" (Col. 1: 27). In this age, we now suffer with Christ
"in order that we may also be glorified with him" (Rom. 8: 17).
God has called us "into his own kingdom and glory" (1 Thess.
2: 12). Christians have received their calling "so that you may
obtain the glory of our Lord Jesus Christ" (2 Thess. 2: 14).
God is preparing for us "an eternal weight of glory beyond all
comparison" (2 Cor. 4: 17). "We rejoice in our hope of sharing
the glory of God" (Rom. 5: 2). At Christ's Parousia, "the
righteous will shine like the sun in the kingdom of their
Father" (Mt. 13: 43).

The significance of such sayings is found in the fact that in
the Old Testament, glory (*kabod*) is the term used to designate
God in his divine splendour, divine power, visible divine
radiance.[25] To cite only one illustration: When Solomon built
a temple for the Lord, after his prayer of dedication, the glory
of the Lord came down and filled the temple, "and the priests
could not enter the house of the Lord, because the glory of the
Lord filled the Lord's house" (2 Chron. 7: 2). "Glory"
throughout the Old Testament often bears this theological
meaning of God in his visible self-manifestation. At the end of
the age, God will manifest his glory as he never has done before,
so that even the order of creation will be transformed into a
new and redeemed order. This is the meaning of the already-
cited verse in Romans 8: 21: "because the creation itself will
be set free from its bondage to decay and obtain the liberty of
the glory of the children of God."

This reflects the basic theology of the entire Bible. The Bible
assumes the existence of two worlds: the visible, natural,
historical world of men, and an invisible, "spiritual" world of
God. Greek thought often felt that man's true home was not
the earth but the invisible, spiritual world which could be

apprehended only by disciplined minds. The good life therefore meant strict control of the bodily passions and the cultivation of the mind. "Salvation" would be achieved by the good man when, at death, he strips off the burdensome body and his soul finds its way to the world of ultimate reality. Much popular Christian faith and some scholarly thinking reflects this pattern.

This is not the biblical theology. The entire Bible assumes that the created world, including man in his bodily existence, is the creation of God and is therefore good. The evil in the world is not intrinsic to its being creation; creation, along with man, has suffered the penalty of man's sin and lies under a curse. Salvation means the visitation of God from the invisible world into the visible world of men.[26] One Old Testament scholar has summed up the Old Testament doctrine of God in the phrase, "the God who comes". God has abandoned neither man nor creation to their fallenness. God visited Abraham in Haran to call him out to be the father of God's people. He visited Moses in the desert to make him the deliverer of his people in Egypt. He visited Israel in her bondage to lead her to the promised land and make her a nation. He visited Israel and Judah in judgment when both nations became sinful and hopelessly apostate. He visited men in the incarnation, when the Word became flesh and dwelt among us both to reveal himself and to rescue fallen man; and he will visit men once again in the Parousia of Christ to finish his work of redemption for the whole of creation. This is why what we call the Second Coming of Christ is absolutely essential in the plan of redemption. "He who began a good work in you will bring it to completion at the day of Jesus Christ" (Phil. 1: 6). Because creation is good, it must be redeemed from the curse of corruption. Because man is God's creation, redemption must mean the resurrection and transformation of his very body. As long as sin, evil, corruption, decay, violence, and death remain in the world, God's redemptive work remains ever incomplete.

This is why the New Testament, particularly John, speaks of the manifestation of God's glory in the earthly ministry of Jesus. "We have beheld his glory, glory as of the only Son from the Father" (Jn. 1: 14). But in the days of his flesh, *the glory was a veiled glory*, evident only to the eyes of faith. When

Jesus changed the water into wine at Cana, John says that Jesus manifested his glory (Jn. 2: 11). But most people did not see it. All the casual observer noticed was particularly good wine. For a moment at the transfiguration, the glory was no longer concealed but shone out so that the three disciples with Jesus were amazed (Lk. 9: 28-36). Although it is beyond human conception, the consummation will be nothing less than a complete redeeming visitation of God in his glory which will mean fearful judgment for the wicked but redemption for those who have loved and served God. In his incarnation, Jesus came from the glory of God (Jn. 17: 5) to bring the glory of God to men in veiled, incarnate form. In his exaltation, he returned to the glory of God (Lk. 24: 26). At his Parousia, he will bring the glory of God to earth with redeeming, transforming power. Then both creation and creatures will share the divine glory.

The entire Bible shows great restraint in its picturing of the future. Sometimes the future is pictured in the Old Testament in very earthly terms; sometimes in terms of a new heaven and a new earth (Isa. 65: 17; 66: 22). But the important fact throughout is the eschatological manifestation of God's glory in redeeming transforming power. The New Testament shows even greater restraint, never speculating about the form or nature of redeemed existence, except to say it will be bodily, earthly existence, transformed by God's glory. Life in the Age to Come is truly indescribable in terms of human, historical categories.

This study of the theological meaning of "glory" provides background and illuminates the stories of Paul's conversion on the Damascus Road (Acts 9: 3-9; 22: 6-16; 26: 12-18). These three stories contain details which do not harmonise with each other, but the main points are clear. Paul saw great light, and out of that light came a voice which identified itself as being that of Jesus. In this experience, the exalted Christ disclosed himself to Paul *in his glory*. One account says that those journeying with Paul saw the light but obviously did not know what to make of it (Acts 22: 9).

Modern scholars who cannot believe the resurrection accounts of the New Testament try to explain Paul's conversion in various ways. Some appeal to Romans 7 finding here an autobiographical account of Paul as a Jew. While appearing to be a proper, proud Pharisee, he was in fact in deep turmoil. He knew that he was not fulfilling the Law's demands; he was conscious of profound sinfulness; he despaired of ever being able to please God. The cry, "Wretched man that I am! Who will deliver me from the body of this death?" (Rom. 7: 24) is his cry of despair of ever fulfilling the Law and so pleasing God. His agony of soul came to an emotional climax on the Damascus Road which resulted in his conversion. It is sometimes said that as a result of listening to Stephen's preaching (Acts 7: 58), Paul was under deep conviction by the Holy Spirit. The words "It hurts you to kick against the goads" (Acts 26: 14) refer in this interpretation to the convicting pressure of the Holy Spirit. Thus Paul's conversion is completely intelligible as a psychological phenomenon.

The trouble with this interpretation is that it is contradicted by Paul's own words. He tells us himself that he lived a life that was blameless in terms of the Law (Phil. 3: 6). He himself claims that even though he tried to destroy the church by persecution, God had mercy on him because he had done it in ignorance (1 Tim. 1: 13). There is every evidence that Paul was sincere in his belief that a crucified Jesus could not possibly be the Messiah, and the church could therefore not possibly be the people of God. The very fact of crucifixion disqualified Jesus from being Messiah, for it was Messiah's role to reign, not to die (see Chapter 6). Only a personal confrontation with Jesus, risen and exalted, could change Paul's mind. It would not be too much to say that Paul's conversion was a psychological miracle. There was no psychological conditioning to prepare him for this experience.

Many scholars are unwilling to accept this interpretation and go to great lengths to explain in natural "historical" terms the Damascus Road experience. A learned Jewish scholar explains Paul's conversion in terms of an epileptic seizure.[27] An American clergyman explains it either in terms of an epileptic seizure or prostration due to the heat of the sun.[28] Another New Testament scholar imagines Paul was caught in a fierce tempest of wind.[29] All such explanations are sheer fantasy. Bultmann writes as though Paul has been confronted by Christian preaching and was brought to decision by it,[30] but there is nothing in Paul's own witness to support this view. All we have is his unqualified statement, "Have I not seen Jesus our Lord?" (1 Cor. 9: 1)—an experience which completely transformed his conduct, revolutionised his thinking, and reversed the whole course of his life. Here is first-hand personal testimony that Jesus was alive. A prominent German Jewish scholar makes the amazing statement, "We must accept fully the real objectivity of the encounter . . . The historian of religion is expected to recognise the faith of Paul in the manifested son of God to be the factual result of his encounter with the crucified and exalted Jesus of Nazareth. Hence he must accept the faith which inspired Paul."[31] If we accept Paul's own testimony, we must conclude that he actually was confronted by the exalted, glorified Jesus. If we do not accept it, we can only plead ignorance to what amounts to a psychological miracle.

We have devoted considerable space to a discussion of the nature of the eschatological resurrection and have found that the saints will enter the Age to Come in bodily form but in glorified, transformed bodies, which are utterly inconceivable to the natural mind. Earthly, historical experience knows nothing and has no analogy for what the New Testament says about the resurrection body. Why have we devoted so much space to the resurrection of believers in the last day? Because it has great relevance for our study of the resurrection of Jesus, for Paul speaks of his resurrection as the *beginning of the eschatological resurrection*. Jesus in his resurrection is "the first fruits of those who have fallen asleep" in death (1 Cor. 15: 20). The term "first fruits" may not be meaningful in a twentieth-century urban society, but in first century Palestine, first fruits meant *the actual beginning of the harvest*. First fruits is more than blossoms with its promise of fruitage; it is more than green fruit with its assurance of a large crop; it was the actual beginning of the harvest itself with the certainty of much more of the same grain shortly to follow. Thus as in Adam, all who are in Adam die, so also in Christ shall all who are in Christ be made alive. "But each in his own order; Christ the first fruits, then at his coming those who belong to Christ" (1 Cor. 15: 23).[32] That is to say: *the resurrection body of Jesus was of the same order as the resurrection bodies of the saints at the end of the age.*

Both Jesus and the saints have a "spiritual body". Both Jesus and the saints have a glorified body. This is most vividly set forth in Philippians 3: 21 which speaks of our present lowly bodies being changed to be like his glorious body.

How did Paul arrive at his concept of the resurrection body as a transfigured "spiritual' body? At this point, Pannenberg offers the suggestion that the Pauline concept is not really original with Paul but presupposes the background of Jewish apocalyptic. Pannenberg appeals primarily to the Apocalypse of Baruch 50-51 where the dead are first raised in the same bodies in which they died so that they might recognise each other, and after that they are transformed into the splendour of angels to enjoy the blessings of "the world which is now invisible" — the paradise that is above.[33] It is beyond question that in Baruch we find the concept of a transformed body; and the present author is convinced in addition to this that Pauline theology stands in continuity with the apocalyptic tradition.[34] However, there are two striking differences that make it difficult to believe that Paul found his concept of a transformed body in a tradition such as that reflected in the Apocalypse of Baruch. First, Baruch has the dead first raised in their natural, physical bodies — an idea which Paul vigorously refutes. Second, the dead are transformed that they may dwell "in the heights of that world . . . , and they shall be made like unto the angels" (Apoc. Bar. 51: 10). This strikes a decidedly different note from Paul. He does not conceive of the saints being transformed to dwell in a heavenly world; he conceives of redeemed existence *on this earth*, transformed by the glory of God (Rom. 8: 21). While there is a somewhat analogous concept in Baruch, the differences are such that we cannot establish dependence.

In any case, even if we assume that the apocalyptic tradition influenced Pauline thought, this would not account for Paul's conversion experience, nor for the resurrection faith. Pannenberg himself admits this:

Now, precisely because the resurrection of a single man was quite unfamiliar to the apocalyptic tradition, we must suppose that a special event underlay the apostolic Easter message, an event that caused so decisive a change in the traditional expectation of the End. Evidently something had happened to the witnesses of the appearances of the Risen One for which their language had no other word than that used to characterise the eschatological expectation, i.e., the resurrection from the dead.[35]

It is far better therefore to conclude, against Pannenburg, that it was Paul's familiarity with the theology of glory, and his experience of meeting Jesus in his glorified state, that led Paul to his theology of glorified bodies in the eschatological resurrection. At least, Philippians 3: 21 suggests this solution—for our lowly body is to be changed "to be like his glorious body".

This is the problem that confronts the historian as historian. Jesus' resurrection body was not of this world; it belonged to the Age to Come. In his resurrection he abolished death and he brought life and immortality to light (2 Tim. 1: 10). Jesus' resurrection body was no longer subject to the natural "laws" of time and space. He had entered the world of God. He belonged to the Age to Come. But what can the historian know of a world to come? What can the historian know of the world of God? What can the historian know of bodies which do not respond to the laws of motion and gravity? These are matters of Christian faith, not of historical investigation. Although it was an event in history, Jesus' resurrection had no antecedent historical cause—a sequence which the historian assumes. Furthermore, the resurrection itself did not mean the revivification of a dead corpse; it meant the radical transformation of the body of Jesus from the world of nature to the world of God. Nature knows of no bodies like Jesus' resurrection body; it was utterly unique. History has no analogy for it. Its character beggars the imagination. This is why many historians believe in the factuality—the eventfulness—the objective reality of the resurrection and yet feel they must say that the resurrection is not "historical" because it utterly transcends all historical experience and knowledge. The resurrection of Jesus is the most decisive point at which the Age to Come broke into this age, in which the supernatural world of God intersected this world. In historical idiom, the Age to Come lies beyond history. It will be a state of existence under the control of altogether different laws than the laws of nature.

This interpretation of Paul agrees with the witness of the Gospels. We have concluded that the stone at the tomb was not moved to let Jesus out; he left the tomb while the stone rested on the door, leaving the grave clothes undisturbed behind him. We concluded that it was not precisely correct to say that Jesus passed through closed doors. Rather, he suddenly appeared to his disciples and then with equal suddenness disappeared. Either this is pure legend, or Jesus' body moved about according to laws that transcend all known laws of space and motion. And this is precisely what Paul says about the nature of the resurrection body.

Now we must deal with a real difficulty. There is admittedly a striking difference between the form of the appearance of Christ to Paul on the Damascus Road and the appearances in the Gospels. Paul encountered Jesus in his *glorified* body. What he saw was a blaze of glory. The voice identified itself as Jesus. In the Gospels, Jesus has a far more flesh-like body which can be not only heard with the ears but also observed with the eyes and felt with the hands. We would not gloss over the difference between Paul and the Gospels; it is real and striking.

Some scholars simply point to these two concepts as contradictory. "The materialising of the bodily aspect which occurs later in levels of the tradition and which makes a recognition through sense perception possible . . . contradicts the essence of the appearances."[36] Pannenberg thinks that *all* of the appearances, including those related in the Gospels, were like the appearance to Paul, which he calls an objective vision.[37] This is a persuasive position, except for one fact: the Gospel tradition was still under the control of eye-witnesses (see above, Chapter 7). While memory will confuse details, particularly details of chronology, it is not likely to confuse such an important matter as this. The experiences of the meetings with Jesus must have been indelibly stamped on the mind. Here we must, as historians, rely on general historical probability. Speaking from the theological point of view, if Jesus had actually entered a new realm of existence at his resurrection, there remains no reason to deny the possibility that he could appear to his disciples in completely human form, as the Gospel witness said he did. We are here dealing with a realm of existence unknown to us. If so, such appearances were condescensions of the risen, exalted Jesus to the obtuseness and unbelief of his disciples.

There remains one final question: that of the relationship between the resurrection and the exaltation of Jesus. The problem which we have just discussed could be answered by insisting that Jesus did not enter his glorified state until the ascension. During the forty days, he was in a different mode of existence which involved a different body than after his ascension when he returned to the world of God and became "a life-giving Spirit". However, the logic of what we found thus far in the witness of both the Gospels and Paul suggests that *the resurrection of Jesus was his exaltation*. At his resurrection he entered the invisible world of God. His appearances to his disciples did not mean the passing of one body through other solid substances; it means that Jesus, who was with them but invisible, made himself visible to their physical senses.

Do we have any exegetical support for this position? Peter in the first recorded sermon after the resurrection seems to identify the resurrection and the exaltation. "This Jesus God raised up, and of that we all are witnesses. Being therefore exalted at the right hand of God . . ." (Acts 2: 32-33). This same pattern appears in Acts 5: 30-31: "The God of our fathers raised Jesus whom you killed by hanging him on a tree. God exalted him at his right hand as Leader and Saviour." Resurrection and ascension are conflated in Colossians 3: 1: "If then you have been raised with Christ, seek the things that are above, where Christ is, seated at the right hand of God." In the great Christological passage in Philippians 2, there is in fact no mention of the resurrection. Jesus "became obedient unto death, even death on a cross. Therefore God has highly exalted him and bestowed on him the name that is above every name" (Phil. 2: 8-9). In a similar way, Hebrews moves directly from death to exaltation: "When he had made purification for sins, he sat down at the right hand of the majesty on high" (Heb. 1: 3). In Hebrews, there are numerous references to Jesus' exaltation (1: 13; 8: 1; 10: 12; 12: 2) but only one reference to the resurrection as such (13: 20). Luke-Acts alone emphasises the ascension as an event separate from the resurrection. If our view of the authorship of Luke-Acts is correct (see Chapter 7), Luke must have

obtained information about the forty days of Jesus' appearances
(Acts 1:3) and writes reliable history; however, even Luke
does not identify the ascension with the exaltation; the story
is told with no elaboration as to its meaning.

If the exaltation took place at the resurrection, what is the
meaning of the ascension? It is merely to signal the end of
Jesus' resurrection appearances. He appeared only once after
the forty days, but this was in an abnormal situation.

In all fairness, it should be pointed out that this is by no
means the universal opinion among contemporary scholars.
Some urge that the bodily nature of Jesus' resurrection demands
the ascension, for it would be inappropriate for Jesus to remain
permanently on earth.[38] Others urge that the ascension is the
taking of his redeemed humanity into heaven.[39] However,
such positions are fraught with problems. We have seen that
the *resurrection itself* was an eschatological event—the first fruits
of the resurrection at the end of the age. There is strong reason
to believe from Paul that the resurrection was Jesus' entrance
into the life of the Age to Come—i.e., exalted, glorified
existence. It was the emergence of eternal life in the world of
mortality. Other positions are faced with two difficult questions:
What was the difference between Jesus' resurrected body and
his glorified body received at the ascension? And where was
Jesus during the forty days when he was absent from his
disciples? The position we have expounded does not need to
answer these questions. Jesus was with them, but unseen.

To be sure, Acts describes the ascension as a going up from
earth to heaven; and this suggests a three-decker world with
heaven a literal astronomical place above the atmosphere.
However, if heaven, understood as the world of God, is a
realm of existence other than and different from the physical
universe, there is no other way Jesus could have signalled his
final disappearance into that other realm than by a visible
ascension such as Luke describes. It is doubtful that Luke was
thinking in cosmological terms. He was describing the cessation
of the resurrection appearances of Jesus—"an acted declaration
of finality".[40]

What then did Jesus mean when he said to Mary, "Touch
me not, for I am not yet ascended to my Father" (Jn. 20:17,
A.V.)? Many scholars see in this saying a reference to an

ascension prior to the one related by Luke-Acts. However, there is really no problem with this verse. The Authorised Version does not accurately render the Greek verb. The R.S.V. renders it, "Do not hold me", and the N.E.B. does even better with the translation, "Do not cling to me". Mary, upon recognition of Jesus, had apparently, like the women in Matthew 28: 9, tried to seize Jesus in a clasp of loving embrace as though she would never let him get away from her again. Jesus merely replies, "You do not need to hold on to me, I haven't left you yet." There is therefore no contradiction whatever between Jesus' prohibition to Mary and his permission to Thomas to touch his scars (Jn. 20: 27). Mary needed to learn that Jesus in his resurrection was establishing a new relationship with his disciples; Thomas needed to learn that it was actually Jesus risen from the dead. The motifs of the two incidents are quite different.

We conclude, then, that the witness of the Gospels and the witness of Paul are in *substantial* agreement. Neither of them represent the resurrection of a dead corpse to physical, earthly life. Both Paul and the Gospels, though admittedly in different ways, describe the resurrection in terms of continuity of person and personality but discontinuity in the relationship of the resurrection body to the physical body. Such is the witness of the New Testament. What is the historian to make of this witness?

NOTES

1. Hans von Campenhausen, "The Events of Easter and the Empty Tomb," *Tradition and Life in the Church* (Philadelphia: Fortress, 1968), p. 44.
2. See W. A. Beardslee, "James," *Interpreter's Dictionary of the Bible*, E–J, p. 793.
3. F. F. Bruce, *1 and 2 Corinthians* (London: Oliphants, 1971), p. 141.
4. *Ibid.*, p. 139. See also W. Künneth, *The Theology of the Resurrection* (London: S.C.M., 1965), p. 94; J. A. T. Robinson, "Resurrection in the NT," *Interpreter's Dictionary of the Bible*, R–Z, p. 45; C. K. Barrett, *The First Epistle to the Corinthians* (New York: Harper & Row, 1968), p. 340; Reginald Fuller, "The Resurrection of Jesus Christ," *Biblical research* 4 (1960), p. 12.

5. See above, Ch. 6.

6. See above, p. 46.

7. See p. 47.

8. The Targum (Aramaic translation) of this passage reads, "He will raise us in the days of consolation which shall come in the future; on the day of the resurrection of the dead he will raise us up that we may live before him."

9. See M. C. Tenney, *The Reality of the Resurrection* (New York: Harper & Row, 1963), p. 44.

10. See Vincent Taylor, *The Gospel according to St. Mark* (London: Macmillan, 1952), p. 378.

11. G. Delling in G. Kittel's *Theological Dictionary of the New Testament*, VIII, p. 220. See also G. Delling in *The Significance of the Message of the Resurrection for Faith in Jesus Christ*, ed. by C. F. D. Moule (Naperville: Allenson, 1968), p. 80.

12. J. Schneider in Kittel's *Dictionary*, II, p. 466. The New English Bible renders it, "Though this birth of mine was monstrous," the idea being, apparently, that the half-formed foetus in a miscarriage is an undeveloped, repulsive thing.

13. W. Pannenberg, *Jesus—God and Man* (Philadelphia: Westminster, 1968), p. 93. Incidentally, Pannenberg argues strongly for the empty tomb but he does not explain the significance of that fact. Michael Perry in his interesting book, *The Easter Enigma* (London: Faber and Faber, 1959), also accepts the facticity of the empty tomb. He devotes the second half of his book to the exposition of "a telepathetic theory of the resurrection appearances".

14. F. F. Bruce, *op. cit.*, p. 142.

15. A. Oepke in Kittel's *Dictionary*, II, p. 539; W. F. Arndt and F. W. Gingrich, *A Greek-English Lexicon of the New Testament* (Chicago: University Press, 1957), p. 260; C. F. D. Moule, *An Idiom-Book of New Testament Greek* (Cambridge: University Press, 1953), p. 76; F. Blass, A. Debrunner, and R. W. Funk, *A Greek Grammar of the New Testament* (Chicago: University Press, 1961), p. 118.

16. W. Michaelis in Kittel's *Dictionary*, V, p. 359.

17. *Ibid.*, p. 357.

18. See F. F. Bruce, "Paul on Immortality," *Scottish Journal of Theology* 24 (1971), pp. 457–472.

19. This is worked out in detail by the present author in *Jesus and the Kingdom* (London: S.P.C.K., 1966), pp. 111ff.; *The Presence of the Future* (Grand Rapids: Eerdmans, 1974, 2nd ed.), pp. 115ff.

20. Oscar Cullmann, *Christ and Time* (Philadelphia: Westminster, 1964; revised edition).

21. Hebrews 2:14 states this in language even more explicit than Paul's.

22. The present author has worked this out in *Jesus and the Kingdom*, pp. 55–60; *The Presence of the Future*, pp. 59–64.

23. See G. E. Ladd, *Jesus and the Kingdom*, pp. 185ff.; *The Presence of the Future*, pp. 189ff.

24. See p. 45.

25. See the excellent study of G. Kittel in Kittel's *Theological Dictionary* II, pp. 247–251.

26. This thesis is worked out by the present author in his book, *The Pattern of New Testament Truth* (Grand Rapids: Eerdmans, 1968).

27. Joseph Klausner, *From Jesus to Paul* (London: Allen & Unwin, 1944), p. 329.

28. A. Powell Davies, *The First Christian* (New York: Farrar, Straus, and Cudahy, 1957), p. 27.

29. Emil G. Kraeling, *I Have Kept the Faith* (Chicago: Rand, McNally, 1965), p. 50.

30. R. Bultmann, *Existence and Faith*, ed. by Schubert Ogden (New York: Meridian Books, 1960), p. 115.

31. H. J. Schoeps, *Paul* (London: Lutterworth, 1961), p. 55.

32. For our present purpose, we need not discuss whether "the end" in verse 24 means the end of the resurrection or the end of the age.

33. See above, pp. 53f. for the eschatology of the Apocalypse of Baruch.

34. See G. E. Ladd, "The Relevance of Apocalyptic for New Testament Theology," in *Reconciliation and Hope* (Leon Morris Festschrift. London: Paternoster, 1974).

35. Wolfhart Pannenberg, "The Revelation of God in Jesus," in *Theology as History*, ed. by J. M. Robinson & J. B. Cobb, Jr. (New York: Harper & Row, 1967), p. 115.

36. Leonhard Goppelt, *Apostolic and Post-Apostolic Times* (New York: Harper & Row, 1970), p. 19. Goppelt does, however, believe that Jesus rose in bodily form.

37. W. Pannenberg, *Jesus—God and Man*, p. 93.

38. Bruce Metzger, "The Ascension of Jesus Christ," *Historical and Literary Studies* (Grand Rapids: Eerdmans, 1968), p. 84.

39. C. F. D. Moule, "The Ascension," *Expository Times* 68 (1956–57), p. 208. See also A. W. Argyle, *ET* 66 (1954–55), p. 240.

40. C. F. D. Moule, *op. cit.*, p. 208.

CHAPTER 10

"Historical" Explanations

IN THE TWO PRECEDING CHAPTERS, on the witness of the Gospels and of Paul, we have been working as a biblical exegete trying to understand in terms of themselves what these two witnesses mean to say. We have concluded that both the Gospels and Paul mean to say that Jesus was raised from the dead not merely to return to physical, historical life, but was raised into the world of God—indeed, into the Age to Come. He convinced his disciples that he was alive again, although in a new and different form of being, by appearances in bodily form to the disciples, and in a vision of glory to Paul. We have admitted that both the resurrection itself and the resurrection appearances are not technically historical in the sense that they can be explained in terms of historical causality and analogy. They can only be explained in terms of the world of God which transcends all historical reality, even though the Bible witnesses to the fact that God's world can act and interact with history.

What then is the historian to do as a historian? We have argued that there are several strictly historical facts which the historian must try to explain. These are: the fact that a dying and rising Messiah was utterly unexpected; the fact that Jesus was dead; the fact that he was buried; the fact that the disciples were disheartened and discouraged; the fact that on Easter Sunday the tomb was found empty; the fact of the undisturbed grave clothes; the fact that the disciples had certain experiences which they interpreted in terms of the person of Jesus, thus giving rise to the resurrection faith; the fact of the rise of a new movement based on the belief that Jesus was alive; the fact of the conversion of Paul. The historian must try to account for the facts of history.

There are two approaches one can take. One is the historical-critical view which assumes in advance that history is a closed continuum of historical causes and effects (see Chap. 1). This approach eliminates for *a priori* reasons the possibility that *God* raised Jesus from the dead. God by definition is the wholly other who does not interfere—indeed cannot interfere in the closed nexus of historical events. This approach must look elsewhere than to God to find the cause of the rise of the resurrection faith. This chapter is concerned with such strictly "historical" explanations. This approach is obviously closed-minded to one possible explanation of the resurrection faith: that God actually raised Jesus.

A different approach is what we may call the inductive approach. Science works by facts, and is open-minded to all hypotheses which may explain the facts. The inductive approach considers all possible explanations and selects the hypothesis which best accounts for the known historical facts. One could argue that this approach is more open-minded than the historical-critical approach and is therefore more truly scientific. At least, it does not close its mind to one possible explanation before the evidence is heard.

In this chapter, we wish to examine the several strictly historical approaches to test their viability in comparison with the hypothesis that God raised him from the dead.

The most ancient "historical" explanation for the admitted facts that cluster around the resurrection is that the disciples stole the body of Jesus and then perpetrated the fraud that Jesus had risen from the dead. This view is found in New Testament times. Matthew records that the elders gave money to the soldiers who guarded the tomb and said, "Tell the people, 'His disciples came by night and stole him away while we were asleep'" (Mt. 28: 13). This explanation was also reflected in Origen's debate with Celsus in the early third century A.D.[1] Origen disposes of this fanciful explanation by arguing that men do not risk losing their lives in defence of a lie.

This explanation has been defended in modern times by a

German scholar named H. M. Reimarus. In 1778 he published a work entitled *The Goal of Jesus and His Disciples*.[2] He argues that the disciples after Jesus' death were unwilling to abandon the kind of life they had led with Jesus. So they stole the body of Jesus and hid it, and proclaimed to all the world that he would soon return as the Messiah. However, they waited for fifty days before making this announcement in order that the body, if it should be found, would be unrecognisable.

Origen's answer still stands. Men do not risk their lives and suffer martyrdom (Acts 7:60; 12:2) for a lie.

A second and equally implausible effort to explain the rise of the resurrection faith is the "swoon theory" which was propounded by another German scholar by the name of Paulus. In 1828, he published a life of Christ in which he explained the "resurrection" of Jesus in terms of his non-death. Paulus points out that crucifixion was usually a slow, protracted dying, and cases are on record of victims who were crucified, taken down from the cross alive, and survived. Jesus "died" in an amazingly short time. The loud cry he uttered shortly before his "death" shows that his strength was far from exhausted. His "death" was only a death-like trance. The thrust of the spear in Jesus' side was no more than a surface wound. However, Jesus appeared to have expired and so was taken down from the cross and laid in the tomb. The cool grave and the aromatic spices contributed to the process of resuscitation, and finally the storm and the earthquake roused Jesus to full consciousness. The earthquake also had the effect of rolling the stone away from the entrance to the tomb. Jesus stripped off the grave clothes, and put on a gardener's outfit he managed to procure. That is why Mary mistook him for the gardener (Jn. 20:15).

If there is any plausibility about such a theory, one must assume that Jesus lived out the remainder of his days in hiding. While the disciples were challenging the leaders of Judaism with the proclamation that Jesus was living and his Kingdom coming, Jesus himself was in solitary retreat, probably unknown to his closest disciples. Such a view is utterly incredible.

Nevertheless, a modern version of the "swoon theory" is defended in a book by a competent biblical scholar. Hugh Schonfield's *The Passover Plot*,[3] backed by a vigorous promotion programme of public appearances, television and radio interviews, sold scores of thousands of copies. The book is a tissue of imagination. Jesus felt himself called as a prophet to preach repentance in Israel. However his mission did not succeed. From a study of the Old Testament scriptures, Jesus became convinced that he should suffer atonement for the sins of his people. So Jesus formed a deliberate plot to bring about the sufferings of crucifixion but not death. He provoked Judas to betray him to the council, who in turn handed him over to Pilate under the accusation of political sedition. The "blasphemy" Jesus uttered (Mk. 14: 64) was against Caesar, not God. Jesus so cleverly plotted that he brought about his crucifixion at the hands of Pilate on Friday, in the confident expectation that his body would not be left on the cross beyond sunset of the sabbath. Indeed, he plotted with Joseph of Arimathea to arrange for his death and "resurrection". At a given signal, "I thirst", an emissary of Joseph administered a powerful drug on a sponge to Jesus which immediately sent him into a death-like trance; but he was not dead. Joseph rushed to Pilate to ask for Jesus' body, and was granted his request. Joseph promptly took down the body and laid it in a tomb. Jesus had planned his "resurrection", i.e., that he would revive and rejoin his disciples. But an unforeseen incident occurred: while he was still on the cross, Jesus' side was pierced by a soldier's lance. This added to his weakness. In any case, he was taken from the tomb after a few hours; Jesus begged his friends to deliver a message to his disciples that he would meet them in Galilee. But it was not to be. On the contrary, he expired and was laid in an unknown tomb, leaving the original tomb empty with the wrappings neatly folded. Peter and John came to the tomb, and suddenly it came to John that Jesus had risen. Mary also came to the garden—"unbalanced" Mary in a "half-crazed" condition. She saw a figure near the tomb—either the gardener or the man who had assisted Joseph. She identified him as Jesus. The two disciples on the Emmaus road met a stranger and later concluded that it was Jesus.

This is obviously a highly imaginative piece of fiction which runs entirely contrary to the witness of the gospels. Schonfield ignores altogether the witness of Paul, which, critically speaking, is our most important witness. He does not try to explain how Jesus could have "appeared" to five hundred brethren at once. Furthermore, this makes Jesus into a pious fraud. It is discouraging that such a fictitious story could capture the imagination of the public as this book did—and all in the name of scholarship.

Another famous Harvard scholar, at the time at Leiden, Kirsopp Lake, wrote a book on *The Resurrection of Jesus Christ*.[4] In discussing the "facts behind the tradition", he suggests that in the area where Jesus was buried were several tombs. The women, visiting the tomb early on Sunday morning, were not sure of the correct tomb and therefore came upon one that was empty. A young man stood at the entrance, and guessing their errand, tried to tell them that they had made a mistake in the place. "He is not here", he said, "see the place where they laid him," and probably pointed to the next tomb. The women were frightened at the detection of their errand and fled, only imperfectly or not at all understanding what they had heard. Later on, they came to believe that the young man was something more than they had seen, that he was announcing Jesus' resurrection.

These first four "historical" explanations of the resurrection faith need little refutation. They are not based on the facts of the New Testament. It is historically possible, of course, that the empty tomb can be explained by the theory that Jesus' body had been removed.[5] This we admit. But the New Testament does not witness to the fact that the empty tomb gave rise to faith. It was—with the exception of John—the *appearances* which evoked faith. There are only two reasonable "historical" hypotheses: the subjective hypothesis theory and the objective hypothesis theory. Many scholars have held that the disciples really did see something, but this something was purely subjective. This possibility must be considered for *visions are real phenomena*. They may be purely subjective, having no corresponding objective reality, but to the person experiencing them, visions are intensely real.

Bultmann has espoused this explanation. "The historian can perhaps to some extent account for that faith [in the resurrection] from the personal intimacy which the disciples had enjoyed with Jesus during his earthly life and so reduce the resurrection appearances to a series of subjective visions."[6] However, it seems obvious that Bultmann himself is not entirely satisfied with the subjective vision hypothesis. Thielicke quotes him as saying, "A vision is never purely subjective. It always has an objective basis. In the vision the encounter which precedes it attains fruition, so that the vision itself became a further encounter . . . It is foolish to regard dreams and visions as subjective experiences. They are in a real sense objective encounters."[7] Yet again, Bultmann appears uncomfortable with such explanations for in a later writing he says, " . . . how the Easter faith arose in individual disciples, has been obscured in the tradition by legend and is not of basic importance."[8] Here is an utterly amazing assertion: it is not important to understand what happened in an event which has influenced the entire culture of the western world more than any other single event!

The subjective vision theory has been eloquently defended by Johannes Weiss. He writes that "the appearances were not external phenomena but were merely the goals of an inner struggle in which faith won the victory over doubt . . . The appearances were not the basis of their faith, though so it seemed to them, so much as its product and result". A faith which could be awakened only by objective appearances "would not possess very much in the way of moral or religious value". Instead of "faith rendered compulsory by miracle, we have to do with a profound inner conviction which through an overwhelming final experience emerges at last into certainty and reality".[9]

A variant of this is that the impact Jesus made on his disciples could not die. So Morton Enslin writes in his recent *The Prophet from Nazareth*:

Who will find it incredible that during those days in Galilee, when everything was alive and vibrant with him, where uppermost in their minds were the memories of what he had said, what he had done, that gradually the first grief and shock gave way and in their place there arose the inevitable confidence that he had not been—could not have been—thwarted.[10]

However, both the subjective vision theory and the personality influence theory are contradicted by the historical data of the gospels. Subjective visions are real phenomena, but they require a certain conditioning to be experienced. These conditions did not prevail. *Faith did not create the appearances; the appearances created faith.* It is too much to say that such miraculous appearances *compelled* faith. However, it is the uniform witness of the New Testament that *something happened to create faith*. It is often contended that Jesus is never said to have appeared to unbelievers, only to believers. This simply is not true on two scores. The disciples were not believers after Jesus' death and burial; and James and Paul never had been disciples; they were both unbelievers when Jesus appeared to them.

The subjective vision theory was long ago exploded by William Milligan.[11] In addition to the fact that the vision theory is inconsistent with the mental state of the disciples, he points out that such visions are not witnessed by five hundred persons at once, that such visions are not extended over a period of forty days, that such visions do not occur only to cease with abrupt suddenness. These arguments have been recently revived by Pannenberg, who firmly rejects the subjective vision hypothesis.[12]

There remains only the "objective vision" theory. Pannenberg appeals to this, arguing that Paul saw a vision of light which was seen by no one else. Pannenberg insists that all of the appearances must have been of the same sort. However, we do not know that what Paul saw was visible to him alone. He nowhere discusses the nature of the appearances. Acts 26: 13 says that Paul's travelling companions also saw the light—but presumably did not know what to make of it. It may not be incorrect to call this a vision; but we should again remember that Paul clearly differentiates between this appearance of Jesus and his visions of heavenly things (2 Cor. 12: 1-4). The thing to remember is that Paul is convinced that he saw the person and heard the voice of the exalted Jesus. It does no harm to call this a vision, as Pannenberg does.

However, it does not follow that *all* of the appearances were of this order. This is contradicted by the witness of the Gospels. Admittedly, one will probably solve this problem in terms of his view of the nature of the Gospels. If the Gospels embody a free-floating tradition which was written down two generations or more after the events they record, this is a plausible argument. But if our view of the Gospels is accurate (see Chapter 7), that they were written in about a single generation after the events they record while eye-witnesses were still available, the appearances of Jesus as recorded in the Gospels must embody a trustworthy memory.

Michael Perry tries to explain the resurrection appearances in terms of psychic phenomena. He writes:

> Jesus . . . communicated with his disciples—we do not know how, so we call it "telepathy"—and caused their minds to project an apparition of his body as they had known it. This would demonstrate to them, in the only way in which they could understand, that it was really he who was teaching them and that he had truly conquered the powers of Death.[13]

A curious feature of his book is that he insists on the empty tomb, but admits that the telepathic theory has nothing to do with the tomb.[14] He goes on to speak of the body of Jesus being withdrawn into a fourth or higher dimension, "ready for reintroductions into our space-time as and when necessary,"[15] and of the "dematerialisation" of the body of Jesus. However, he flatly denies that it was the actual risen body of Jesus which appeared to the disciples.[16]

While this is an intriguing book, its thesis falls far short of demonstration, and there is really no light shed on the problem of the resurrection from alleged analogous experiences in parapsychology.[17] There can be little question but that both Paul and the Gospels believe that Jesus appeared in bodily form.[18] Parapsychology is not an established scientific discipline from which well-established scientific facts can be deduced to explain the resurrection appearances. As a "scientific" explanation, it must be reckoned to be inadequate.

All of these hypotheses which have been put forth to explain the rise of the resurrection faith must be found wanting. The only hypothesis which adequately explains the "historical" facts, including the empty tomb, is that God actually raised the body of Jesus from the realm of mortality in the world of time and space to the invisible world of God, and that Jesus was able to appear to his disciples in different ways on different occasions. Admittedly, this is not a "historical" explanation; it involves *theology*—a belief in God.

Why should I believe in such a God? The answer to this question is older than the Reformation. I believe in the living God because I have met him through the witness of the Holy Scriptures empowered by the Holy Spirit. In the end, I accept the biblical witness to the resurrection not because of logical proof or historical reasoning, but because of an inner quality of the gospel, namely, its truthfulness. It so overpowers me that I am rendered willing to stake the rest of my life on that message and live in accordance with it. My faith is not faith in history but faith in the God who acts in history. It is faith in God who has revealed himself to me in the life and death of Jesus of Nazareth, and in his resurrection, who continues to speak to me through the prophetic word of the Bible.

Does such faith mean a "leap in the dark"? Does historical reasoning have no place in my experience? By no means. For in fact, only the "hypothesis" of actual bodily resurrection adequately explains the known historical facts. *The only reason for not accepting the "biblical hypothesis" is the conviction that it cannot be true*—i.e., to have a closed mind to a real possibility. But "historical reasoning" has not provided an adequate explanation for the rise of the resurrection faith. Therefore, historical reasoning reinforces my Christian convictions, if it does not prove them. There must be critical interaction between my Christian faith and my historical critical faculties. The present author is ready to admit that if historians came up with a completely convincing "historical" explanation of the resurrection faith, his evangelical faith would be shaken. However, it is a kind of negative apologetic that the historian as historian cannot explain what happened, and the best—although amazing—explanation is that of Bultmann: we do not know—and it does not matter.[19] But it *does* matter. Surely, it matters greatly to explain the event which has completely altered the entire course of western history.

At this point, Helmut Thielicke offers a fruitful suggestion. He expounds the necessity of historical research in terms of *anticriticism*.

Even if historical research cannot be considered the critical surveyal of a territory upon which faith could settle down, *it does have the task of determining whether the results of historical criticism contradict the Easter faith or whether they do not* [italics ours]. Naturally, nothing can be the object of our faith which stands in evident contradiction to the factual ... The Easter faith would then be possible only by means of a schizophrenia of our human consciousness—which would be unbearable and unallowable.[20]

Such has been the purpose of this book: to mark out the limitations of historical knowledge; to insist that *something happened* to produce the set of historical facts available to us; and to argue that the only rational explanation for these historical facts is that God raised Jesus in bodily form from the realm of mortality into the world of God. For those who believe in such a God and such a world, this is the only adequate explanation.

NOTES

1. See Origen, *Against Celsus*, II, LVI.
2. Recently translated by G. W. Buchanan (Leiden: Brill, 1970).
3. New York: Bernard Geis, 1965.
4. London: Williams & Norgate, 1912.
5. J. Klausner believes that Joseph removed the body. *Jesus of Nazareth* (New York: Macmillan, 1925), p. 357.
6. Rudolf Bultmann in *Kerygma and Myth*, ed. by H. W. Bartsch (London: S.P.C.K., 1953), p. 42.
7. *Op. cit.*, p. 152.
8. Rudolf Bultmann, *Theology of the New Testament* (New York: Scribners Sons, 1951), I, p. 45.
9. Johannes Weiss, *Earliest Christianity* (New York: Harper and Brothers, 1959), I, p. 30.
10. Morton Enslin, *The Prophet from Nazareth* (New York: McGraw-Hill, 1961), p. 213.
11. William Milligan, *The Resurrection of Our Lord* (New York: Macmillan, 1927), pp. 81–114.
12. Wolfhart Pannenberg, *Jesus—God and Man* (Philadelphia: Westminster, 1968), pp. 85ff.
13. Michael Perry, *The Easter Enigma* (London: Faber & Faber, 1959), p. 195.
14. *Op. cit.*, p. 218.

15. *Op. cit.*, p. 220.
16. *Op. cit.*, p. 198.
17. This is the conclusion of the review by W. A. Whitehouse in the *Journal of Theological Studies* II (1960), p. 237.
18. Pannenberg also appeals to advances in the field of parapsychology to validate his view of the appearances as objective visions. *Op. cit.*, p. 95.
19. See above, p. 24.
20. See Helmut Thielicke, in *The Easter Message Today* (London and New York: Thomas Nelson, 1964), p. 82.

CHAPTER 11

Does it Matter?

AFTER ALL, why does the resurrection have so much importance for Christian faith? Even if Jesus did not rise from the dead, is the essential truth of Christianity impaired? Does there not remain the same God, the same Jesus with his wonderful words, his marvellous teaching, his sacrificial death? Why is the resurrection so very important?

Paul seems to hang the entire corpus of Christian truth on the factuality of the resurrection.

> If Christ has not been raised, then our preaching is vain and your faith is vain. We are found to be misrepresenting God, because we testified of God that he raised Christ, whom he did not raise if it be true that the dead are not raised . . . If Christ has not been raised, your faith is futile, and you are still in your sins. Then those who have fallen asleep in Christ have perished. (1 Cor. 15: 14-18.)

This seems like an exaggerated statement. Does one's belief in God depend on a single event—the resurrection of Jesus? Can one not doubt that such a resurrection is possible and yet believe in God who is creator and sustainer of the world? After all, Holy Scripture says that "whoever would draw near to God must believe that he exists and that he rewards those who seek him" (Heb. 11: 6).

However, Paul says that if Jesus is not raised, we are misrepresenting God. As a matter of fact, the entire Bible is misrepresenting God. It is an emphasis of much modern biblical theology that God has revealed himself through his acts in history. It is widely recognised that revelation in history is one of the most distinctive things about biblical religion. Scholastic orthodoxy may limit God's revelation to the Scriptures as the Word of God and define revelation as the communication from God to man of divine truth. However, God reveals more than truth to men; he reveals *himself*; and this revelation occurred before there was any written word of Scripture. God disclosed himself through his mighty acts.[1] But the deed was always accompanied by the prophetic word. Throughout the history of Israel, God raised up prophets to interpret what God was doing in history. The deliverance from Egypt was due not to the strength of Israel, nor to the skill and cleverness of Moses; it was an act of God. The overthrow of Israel by Assyria and Judah by Babylon was not simply the clash of nationalisms; it was the judgment of God. God's most eloquent word was spoken in the historical event of Jesus of Nazareth. "In many and various ways God spoke of old to our fathers by the prophet; but in these last days he has spoken to us by a Son" (Heb. 1: 1-2).

But if Jesus is not raised, redemptive history ends in the *cul-de-sac* of a Palestinian grave. Then God is not the living God, nor is he the God of the living as Jesus said (Mk. 12: 27). Death is stronger than God; death is stronger than God's word. God's acts are proven futile in the face of man's greatest enemy—death. One may not discount the resurrection, and accept the Bible's witness to redemptive history.

Furthermore, if Jesus' career ended in a tomb, the claims that he made during his earthly ministry are given the lie. He preached the Kingdom of God. This was his central message. It is widely recognised that the meaning of the "Kingdom of God" is God's kingly rule (see Lk. 19: 11-12). When we pray "thy Kingdom come", we are praying that God will manifest his kingly power, destroy his enemies, purge all evil from his universe, and reign in righteousness and peace over a redeemed people. This hope of the establishment of God's Kingdom is the central theme of the prophets.[2] It was also the central theme of Jesus' proclamation. He looked forward to an eschatological day when God would act in his regal power to establish his rule in the earth. At this point, Jesus shared the hope of the apocalyptists,[3] for both were based squarely upon the Old Testament prophetic hope.

However, Jesus taught that this same God had acted in advance of the Day of the Lord in his own person and mission to defeat the spiritual powers of evil by the power of his divine kingly rule to bring the blessings of his Kingdom to men in the midst of history. "If it is by the Spirit of God that I cast out demons, *then the kingdom of God has come upon you*" (Mt. 12: 28). Thus the Kingdom has two moments: an apocalyptic coming at the end of history, and a proleptic coming in the midst of history.[4]

Corresponding to this, Jesus' mission is to be fulfilled in two events. He will come as the heavenly Son of Man as predicted in Daniel 7 to sit in judgment on the world and to establish the Kingdom of God in apocalyptic power. One of the main themes of the parables of the Kingdom in Mark 4 — Matthew 13 is the coming of the Son of Man in glory at the day of judgment to gather the righteous under God's kingly rule. But before he is to accomplish this mission, Jesus has come among men as the Son of Man to fill the role of the Suffering Servant of Isaiah 53 to redeem his people through a ministry of suffering. "For the Son of Man also came not to be served but to serve, and to give his life as a ransom for many" (Mk. 10: 45). This is the truly unique factor in Jesus' message and mission: that the glorious rule of God, which is to be established with power at the end of history has come into history in the lowly Son of Man to achieve its victory through suffering and death. In some way which Jesus did not explain, his triumphant return as the glorious Son of Man was made possible only by his sufferings and death. This is the meaning of the "must". "The Son of Man *must* suffer many things" (Mk. 8: 31). The Christian life, from one point of view, can be considered as the enjoyment of the blessings which Jesus brought to men in his earthly mission.

But if Jesus is dead[5], his entire message is negated. If he is dead, he cannot come in his Kingdom. If he is dead, the hope of a triumphant coming of the heavenly Son of Man is obviously impossible. Furthermore, Jesus' teaching about the presence of the Kingdom and its blessings is also a delusion,

for the presence of the Kingdom-blessings was but an anticipation of the eschatological Kingdom to be established by the
heavenly Son of Man. It is impossible to separate the present
blessings from the future consummation, for the former are
but a proleptic experience of the latter. If Jesus is dead,
his entire message about the Kingdom of God is a delusion.

If Jesus is dead, the heart of New Testament Christology is
also a delusion. The central confession of the early church was
not the saviourhood of Jesus but his Lordship. "If you confess
with your lips that Jesus is Lord,[6] and believe in your heart
that God raised him from the dead, you will be saved"
(Rom. 10: 9). "Let all the house of Israel therefore know
assuredly that God has made him both Lord and Christ
(Messiah), this Jesus whom you crucified" (Acts 2: 36).
"Therefore God has highly exalted him and bestowed on him
the name which is above every name, that at the name of Jesus
every knee should bow, in heaven and on earth and under
the earth, and every tongue confess *that Jesus Christ is Lord*, to
the glory of God the Father" (Phil. 2: 9-11). "For although
there may be so-called gods in heaven or on earth—as indeed
there are many 'gods' and many 'lords'—yet for us there is
one God, the Father . . . and *one Lord, Jesus Christ*" (1 Cor.
8: 6).

Scholars have often called attention to what may seem to be a
disturbing fact—that Paul very infrequently refers to the
historic ministry of Jesus. He is not much concerned about
Jesus' personality, his teachings, his mighty deeds. Paul's
Christology centres almost altogether upon the crucified and
exalted Jesus. Indeed, it is a popular thing with many
"advanced" scholars to argue that Paul *changed* the historical
Jesus into the exalted and glorified Christ. We believe that
Jesus "in the days of his flesh" was already the Son of God;
but he became "the Son of God *in power*" (Rom. 1: 4) at his
exaltation. In any case, Paul's gaze is fixed primarily upon the
exalted Christ who was already the Lord, and who would rule
at God's right hand "until he has put all his enemies under his
feet" (1 Cor. 15: 25).

But this again is a delusion if Jesus is not risen. The New
Testament knows nothing about the persistence of Jesus'
personality apart from the resurrection of the body. Neither

does the New Testament know the "resurrection of the spirit" to heaven such as that found in Enoch. If his body is mouldering in a Palestinian tomb, he cannot be the exalted Lord; he cannot be the victor over his enemies; he cannot destroy his "last enemy"—death—for death has destroyed him. The Christian profession of the Lordship of Christ is a hollow echo.

Paul says that if Christ is not risen, "you are still in your sins". How can this be? Is it not the death of Christ by which atonement is made for our sins? Is not his death efficacious without his resurrection?

Paul says not. Perhaps the best way to expound Paul's thoughts is by dealing with a rather difficult verse. In Romans 4: 25, Paul says that Jesus "was put to death for our trespasses and raised for our justification". The present author has puzzled long over the meaning of this verse. Justification by faith was one of the most important doctrinal themes in Paul's theological thought. Justification means "acquittal". It presupposes the final judgment when all men will stand before God to be judged. There will be a two-fold issue from this judgment: acquitted, or condemned. This two-fold aspect of justification—that it is eschatological and forensic—is clearly illustrated by a saying of Jesus. "On the day of judgment men will render account for every careless word they utter; for by your words you will be justified, and by your words you will be condemned" (Mt. 12: 36). "Careless words" are words uttered when one's guard is down, which reveal the true state of the inner man. In the day of judgment when men will be shown for what they really are, the righteous will be acquitted of all guilt, the wicked will be condemned.

Thus far Paul was at one with Judaism which believed in the acquittal of the righteous in the day of judgment. But here the similarity ceases. The Jews believed that men were righteous because of their good works in obedience to the Law. Paul declares that all are sinners, but because of the death of Christ, sinners who believe in Christ will be justified—indeed, they have already been justified. Paul teaches justification as a present reality grounded in the death of Christ, to be received by sinners by faith (Rom. 3: 21-31).

If their justification is a redemptive work wrought by Christ on his cross, how can Paul say that Christ was raised for our justification? What does resurrection have to do with it?

The answer to this question is that justification is *both* a past event in history and a future eschatological event. It is not the hearers of the Law who will be acquitted but the doers of the Law who *will be* justified (Rom. 2: 13). The temporal orientation of the words, "by one man's obedience many will be made righteous" (Rom. 5: 19), is the future judgment when God will pronounce the verdict of righteousness upon the many. The *"hope* of righteousness" for which we wait is the judicial pronouncement of righteousness, that is, of acquittal in the day of judgment.

This is why Paul says that even believers, who *have been* justified, must appear before the judgment seat of God (Rom. 14: 10), which is also the judgment seat of Christ (2 Cor. 5: 10). The decree of acquittal which was pronounced over us at the cross must be confirmed by God's verdict in the day of judgment. This is the thought behind Romans 8: 33-34: "Who shall bring any charge against God's elect? It is God who justifies; who is to condemn? It is Christ Jesus who died, yes, who was raised from the dead, who is at the right hand of God, who indeed intercedes for us." These words picture the elect-believer on the day of judgment standing before God. God asks, "who can bring any charge that will lead to this man's condemnation?" His enemies, his sins, the devil all speak out with words of condemnation. But that is not the last word. Christ speaks in the believer's defence, recalling that in his suffering and death on the cross, justification was achieved. No voice can prevail over the voice of Christ who defends. But it is not only Jesus who died, but Christ Jesus who was raised from the dead and *who lives to make intercession* to God for the believers. Indeed, we are justified by his resurrection: for if the justification of the cross is a proleptic announcement of the eschatological acquittal, but if Christ has not been raised to defend his people in the eschatological judgment, then the whole doctrine of justification is a figment of the imagination.

The picture we have just painted may seem rather naive; but it requires naive idiom to embody sublime truth.

Finally, Paul hangs the entire eschatological future on the resurrection. "Those who have fallen asleep in Christ have perished" (1 Cor. 15: 18). Upon reflection, this seems to be a rather radical, arbitrary statement coming from Paul, the ex-Pharisee. We have traced the hope of resurrection in Judaism[7] and have found that the idea of eschatology was widespread among the Jews. Luke records that when Paul on his last journey to Jerusalem was brought before the Jewish Sanhedrin, and Paul recognised their hostility to him, he undertook a stratagem which divided the house. "He cried out in the council, 'Brethren, I am a Pharisee, a son of Pharisees; with respect to the hope and the resurrection of the dead I am on trial' " (Acts 23: 6). This statement led to a dissension between the Pharisees and the Sadducees, and the assembly was divided. Luke adds this word of explanation, "for the Sadducees say that this is no resurrection, nor angel, nor spirit; but the Pharisees acknowledge them all" (Acts 23: 8). Why could not Paul have retained his Jewish hope in resurrection even if Christ should be proven to be dead?

However, Paul's words in this passage do not refer to his hope as a Pharisee but to his hope as a Christian. His argument implies that the entire national hope of Israel has now been concentrated in the mission of Jesus, and his examination by the Sanhedrin as a Christian meant in reality an examination of the national hope of Israel. Paul implies here, as he clearly affirms in 1 Corinthians 15: 18, that all hope of resurrection is centred in the person and work of Christ. If Paul is condemned by the Sanhedrin because he believes in Jesus as the Jewish Messiah, the Sanhedrin is in effect denying the hope of resurrection cherished by the Pharisees.

Clearly, Paul's view of Christ contained the conviction that in the mission of Jesus, all the promises of the Old Testament and all the hopes of Israel are concentrated. "For all the promises of God find their yes in him" (2 Cor. 1: 20). The promises of God are no longer merely words, but have become embodied in the historical mission of Jesus. Unto us the ends of the ages have come (1 Cor. 10: 11); i.e., all that God has done and said in former ages has achieved fulfilment in Christ, and believers are heirs of these blessings. Therefore, if Christ is dead, God's promises have died with him. If Christ is dead, the hope of Israel is a futile, empty thing. Therefore, "those who have fallen asleep [believing] in Christ have perished".

This remains fundamental to Christian faith today. When

the present author was a young minister, a very liberal colleague asked him to read a certain book. The course of the argument of the book was that physiology cannot isolate a human soul or say anything about the persistence of personality. The same is true of all the modern sciences; therefore the hope of any sort of immortality is a delusion and a snare.

This remains true. The doctrine of the essential immortality of the soul and its departure at death is a subject for Greek speculation. Apart from the resurrection of Christ, all ideas of life beyond death are empty speculations. When Paul writes to the Ephesians that Gentile pagans are without hope (Eph. 2: 12), he did not mean that they had no idea of a life after death. He did mean that such ideas were human theories in which men could place no confidence. The Christian hope, for Paul, is not a theory or a speculation; it was a certain fact which in turn rested upon another event in history—the resurrection of Jesus from the dead.

Finally, the resurrection of Christ is the only key to the meaning and goal of history. Bultmann is certainly right in saying that an event is known only by its future.[8] That is to say, the meaning of an event cannot be seen in the event itself but in the influence an event has when the event itself has become history. Thus the meaning of history can be seen only when history has reached its goal or destiny. A small segment of history has no meaning in and of itself; its meaning is to be found in its impact upon history and the contribution it makes to the historical process in moving towards its goal.

It is a commonplace among contemporary scholars that of all the religions in the ancient world, only the Hebrew religion was a historical religion. Most ancient religions were essentially nature religions, built upon the recurring cycle of the seasons. Hebrew religion was based on the confidence that God acted in history both to reveal himself and to achieve his redemptive purpose. Because God acted in history, he was the Lord of history and would bring history to the Kingdom of God.[9]

The entire New Testament faith is a further commentary on the Old Testament hope, except for the fact that this hope was revised by the person and mission of Jesus. We have seen that his central message was the Kingdom of God,[10] which means first of all the kingly action of God to establish his reign effectively in all the earth. The goal of history was this eschato-logical Kingdom of God.

Thus Bultmann can say, "the question of meaning in history was raised and answered for the first time within an outlook which believed it knew the end of history. This occurred in the Jewish-Christian understanding of history which was dependent on eschatology. The Greeks did not raise the question of meaning in history, and the ancient philosophers had not developed a philosophy of history. A philosophy of history grew up for the first time in Christian thinking, for Christians believed they knew of the end of the world and of history."[11]

However, Bultmann takes his world-view and his concept of history from the twentieth century and not from the Bible.[12] This leads him to the following conclusion: "Today we cannot claim to know the end and the goal of history. Therefore the question of meaning in history has become meaningless."[13] For Bultmann, all futuristic, realistic eschatology with its teaching of the return of Christ as the glorious Son of Man, the resurrection of the dead, and the establishment of God's Kingdom on earth is mythology which cannot be taken with any degree of literalness. This is why he says that we do not know the goal of history. It certainly cannot be the mythological picture of the Bible. For that matter, the stories about the bodily resurrection of Jesus and his appearances to his disciples are equally mythological. Bultmann does not simply discard such mythology; he "demythologises" it; i.e., he reinterprets it in such a way that it applies to my personal existence. History as such has no meaning, but I can find meaning in my own historicity.

Bultmann has a point. The secular historian surveys history and tries to find patterns of meaning and direction in it, only to fail. Within the confines of his own presuppositions, Bultmann is right. No pattern or direction or goal or meaning can be found within history itself.

What relevance does the resurrection of Christ have for the meaning of history? This may be illustrated by one of the most recent trends in German theology—that which is identified with the name of Wolfhart Pannenberg.[14] Pannenberg agrees that the meaning of history can be known only in terms of the goal of history; and he admits that history can only be seen as a whole from the perspective of its conclusion. The goal of history is the resurrection of the dead. However, the resurrection of the dead has already occurred proleptically in the resurrection of Jesus. With Jesus and his resurrection from the dead, there has already happened what is yet to occur for all other men.[15] Thus Pannenberg conceives of Jesus and his resurrection as the unique event within their history which gives a preview of the future and thus is that which unifies all history.

This is precisely what Paul means by designating the resurrection of Jesus the "first fruits" of the eschatological resurrection at the end of the age. This has led us to designate Jesus' resurrection as an eschatological event. It is an anticipation of the end. To speak crudely, it is a piece of eschatology split off from the end and planted in history. The end has begun; the future is present.

It remains obvious then that if Jesus is not raised from the dead, one can no longer argue from the present to the future. If Jesus is not raised, I know nothing about resurrection at the end of the world. The hope of resurrection, the idea of a world to come, remains theological speculation, with no firm foundation in human experience. History has no meaning, no goal, no purpose. As a human race, we are going nowhere.

However, Paul has himself met the resurrected Jesus, and he knows many others who have had the same experience. Therefore he can write with confidence, "But in fact Christ has been raised from the dead, the first fruits of those who have fallen asleep" (1 Cor. 15: 20).

NOTES

1. See G. Ernest Wright, *God Who Acts* (London: S.C.M., 1952).
2. See John Bright, *The Kingdom of God* (New York: Abingdon-Cokesbury, 1953).
3. See Chapter 5.
4. This is worked out in detail in the author's book, *Jesus and the Kingdom* (London: S.P.C.K., 1966); second edition under the title *The Presence of the Future* (Grand Rapids: Eerdmans, 1974).
5. I recognise that this language will be offensive to some of my colleagues in academia who deny that Jesus rose bodily from the grave but insist that he is very much alive. This position to my mind is illogical

and can only involve some kind of immortality of the spirit, or some hint of a gnostic-like view of the resurrection (2 Tim. 12 : 17). To me, the logic is inescapable: if Jesus did not rise bodily from the grave, he is dead.

6. Notice how the translation of the Authorised Version obscures the meaning of this verse.

7. See Chapter 5.

8. Rudolf Bultmann, *History and Eschatology* (Edinburgh: University Press, 1957), p. 120.

9. See John Bright, *op. cit.*

10. See above, pp. 144f.

11. Rudolf Bultmann, *loc. cit.*

12. See above, p. 25.

13. Rudolf Bultmann, *loc. cit.*

14. See Wolfhart Pannenberg, *Revelation as History* (New York: Macmillan, 1968); *Jesus-God and Man* (Philadelphia: Westminster, 1968).

15. W. Pannenberg, *Revelation as History*, p. 141.

Index